WHAT THE CRITICS HAVE SAID ABOUT "CATHOLIC VIEWPOINT ON CENSORSHIP"

". . . this is the first time that the potentially dangerous censorship controversy has been subjected to courageous definition and analysis."

George N. Shuster, New York *Times Book Review*

"This volume is, in my sober judgment, the single greatest contribution to the problem of censorship over the past decades. . . . This is an admirable book particularly for anti-Catholic bigots, and for men of goodwill it is an invitation to sober thought."

Morris L. Ernst, *Saturday Review*

"Father Gardiner's book is a solid contribution to rational debate. He has performed an important public service in preparing it. I don't know anywhere else where the Catholic viewpoint is expressed so clearly. . . . In doing so, he has served society well. We are all in his debt."

John Cogley, *America*

"I venture to say, most readers, persuaded or not, will never again approach the censorship issue in quite the same way for having been exposed to his [Father Gardiner's] argument; and in this lies the measure of his success."

Thomas B. Leary, *Harvard Law Review*

"This book, which outlines so lucidly the *status questionis*, should be read by everyone, Catholic or Protestant, who is genuinely interested in forming a rational viewpoint on the problem of censorship."

The Sign

"*Catholic Viewpoint on Censorship* seems certain to be read with interest by everyone concerned with the problem of censorship. It is a straightforward presentation, without emotional heat, and in lan~~guage that is not likely to be mis~~understood. Indeed it is an ~~...~~ this vexing question."

D1011868

Rochester Democrat and Chronicle

Harold C. Gardiner, S.J.

CATHOLIC VIEWPOINT
ON CENSORSHIP

REVISED EDITION

IMAGE BOOKS

A Division of Doubleday & Company, Inc.
Garden City, New York

Image Books Edition 1961
by special arrangement with Doubleday & Company, Inc.

Image Books Edition published September, 1961
1st printing .... August, 1961

Imprimi Potest: Thomas E. Henneberry, S.J.
Provincial, New York Province
Society of Jesus

Nihil Obstat: John A. Goodwine, J.C.D.
Censor Librorum

Imprimatur: ✠ Francis Cardinal Spellman
Archbishop of New York
December 31, 1957

The nihil obstat and imprimatur are official declarations that a book or pamphlet is free of doctrinal or moral error. No implication is contained therein that those who have granted the nihil obstat and imprimatur agree with the contents, opinions, or statements expressed.

COVER BY RONALD CLYNE

Copyright © 1958, 1961 by Doubleday & Company, Inc.
Printed in the United States of America
All Rights Reserved

Acknowledgments

Realizations of help that must be gratefully acknowledged crowd in upon one as a book is being readied for the press. I cannot hope to say sufficient thanks to all, but I would like to pay special tribute to a chosen few. First of all, my sincerest thanks to Very Rev. Msgr. Thomas F. Little, Executive Secretary of the National Legion of Decency, and to the Assistant Executive Secretary, Rev. Patrick J. Sullivan, S.J., as well as to Mrs. James F. Looram, Chairman of the Motion Picture Department of the International Federation of Catholic Alumnae. They have been most generous in hearing some of my arguments and lending me the counsel of their wide experience. My thanks, too, for the same kind of help from Very Rev. Msgr. Thomas J. Fitzgerald, Executive Director of the National Office for Decent Literature, and his assistant, John Brennan. I was permitted to examine the files of both organizations.

For permissions to reprint the five appendices, I owe thanks to Rev. Thurston N. Davis, S.J., Editor-in-Chief of *America*, for the two articles that appeared in that review; to John Fischer for his article in *Harper's Magazine*; to Patrick Murphy Malin for the statement of the American Civil Liberties Union and for permission to quote from his personal letter to Father Davis; and to the National Catholic Welfare Conference to reprint the 1957 annual Bishops' Statement. Organizations that favor some forms of censorship and those who oppose censorship have been most frank in supplying information.

My debt to Rev. John Courtney Murray, S.J., goes back over many years during which we have discussed this and similar problems. To all my colleagues on the staff of *America*, my thanks for their patience with my preoccupation while preparing this book; their further patience while perusing it will deepen my indebtedness.

For permission to reprint material as noted below, my thanks are extended to the following publishers:

Harvard University Press for selection from *Free Speech in the United States*, by Zechariah Chafee, Jr.; copyright, 1941, by The President and Fellows of Harvard College.

Little, Brown & Company for selection from *The Public Philosophy*, by Walter Lippmann; copyright, 1955, by Walter Lippmann.

Marquette University Press for selection from *Nature and Func-*

tions of Authority, by Yves Simon; copyright, 1940, by the Aristotelian Society of Marquette University.

Oxford University Press, Inc., for selection from *St. Thomas Aquinas: Philosophical Texts,* by Thomas Gilby.

R. R. Bowker Co. for selection from *The Freedom to Read,* by McKeon, Merton, and Gellhorn; copyright, 1957, by R. R. Bowker & Co.

Charles Scribner's Sons and Sheed & Ward, Ltd. (London), for selection from *Freedom in the Modern World,* by Jacques Maritain.

Contents

8   *Contents*

Introduction

All reviews, lead articles, and editorials in the London *Times Literary Supplement* are unsigned. American custom may or may not approve of this majestic anonymity, but there is little doubt that the very lack of personal identification lends a sort of monumental impressiveness to the dicta of the *Times'* critics. This book can by no means boast of such an Olympian detachment: the course of the discussion will lead, inevitably and perhaps unfortunately, into fields that are booby-trapped to right and to left with controversy. But it may perhaps be good to begin with an observation from the London *Times* which may set the problem in its most general terms.

Reviewing *Man in Contemporary Society: A Source Book Prepared by the Contemporary Civilization Staff of Columbia College, Columbia University, New York* (New York: Columbia University Press, 1957, Vol. II), the *Times* critic states (*Literary Supplement*, June 28, 1957, p. 407):

"The question is commonly raised why the popular press, in spite of its gigantic circulation, has a negligible political influence. The answer is surely that the great questions of policy are of their nature complicated, and if issues are over-simplified so as to make them palatable for mass-circulation, they are necessarily presented in a way that makes their presentation valueless to those who have the responsibilities of decision."

This animadversion on the popularization of political issues certainly applies to the subject matter of this book: censorship. The very word has been so bandied about that it means today anything or nothing. And when it is coupled with some other words—"democratic" or "American" or "constitutional," confusion gets worse confounded.

In an effort to delimit the boundaries of our concern, let us make some distinctions. A censor is primarily one who not only disagrees with something (or someone) but who is able to enforce that disagreement through some channel of authority. I may disagree with your freedom to vote the Radical-Social-Demopublican ticket, but I will not be censoring that freedom until I can do something to prevent your so voting. Until the time I can take practical steps toward prevention, I am criticizing, carping, perhaps, or "crabbing," but not censoring—unless one wants to understand criticism as *being* a form of censorship.

The power to disagree and then enforce that disagreement through some channel of authority—in short, the exercise of control—is, then, the sense in which the word "censorship" will be employed in all that follows. It would truly make for clarity of argument if all—the National Legion of Decency, the National Office for Decent Literature, the American Civil Liberties Union, the American Book Publishers Council, and all agencies concerned in the discussion—would resolve to discard the word "censorship" and adopt the word "control." "Censorship," strictly so called, can be exercised in our American constitutional framework only through legal channels; but control is exercised, and will and must be exercised, through channels that are "extra-legal," though never anti-legal. In other words, the state, through judges and courts, can alone bring censorship to bear on the problem of "indecent" literature and films; but society can and does bring "control" to bear long before the judges and courts can or ought to be called into the dispute.

This is indeed, as we see it and as we shall treat later, one of the weaknesses of the stand of the American Civil Liberties Union, the American Book Publishers Council, and other agencies which are set stoutly against all forms of censorship. They are all too ready to make legal procedure the first court of appeal, when perhaps (please note the "perhaps") judges and courts ought to be the last source of decision. In this connection, let me again quote an anonymous opinion from the London *Times Literary Supplement*. In a roundup of many books on the problem of freedom and security in our modern world (among the books were Alger Hiss's *In the Court of Public Opinion* and Samuel Eliot Morison's *Freedom in Con-*

temporary Society), the reviewer remarks (June 28, 1957, pp. 390–91):

"Inasmuch as a citizen feels he cannot exert any influence on circumstances shaping his life . . . he will effectively die toward his society. The citizenry . . . will suffer a kind of schizophrenia: on the one hand their social instincts will still be urgent, but unsatisfiable; on the other hand, as a human-natural defense-mechanism, they will decry and debunk any form of social activity, for it would identify them with the powers-that-be and imply acquiescence in the various forms of deployment of those powers. . . . Thus . . . arises a vast number of non-citizens, citizens of nothing, attaching no positive value whatever to their society . . . having no emotive affection for it, living as atoms in it, fulfilling the barest minimum of obligations to 'get by,' and generally betraying an 'I couldn't care less' mood. . . . Our Anglo-Saxon forefathers . . . would have called such persons Nithings.

"It is not the least of Clio's ironies that, in the measure of the State's arrogating to itself more responsibility of each citizen's life, so have the citizens' loyalties ebbed away and the whole society has lost coherence."

Social controls are being exercised every day in our society. The advertising copywriter is perhaps one of the most potent controllers of social life in modern times; "pressure groups" exist—and their influence is not always an evil or a suspect one. In one sense it is precisely the interplay of such social forces that gives vitality to a democratic society. If the day ever comes when no group in the United States is passionately interested in a cause dear to its heart—and some of the causes may be foolish and some of the hearts fatuous—then shall we be really threatened with the "conformity" all those opposed to any form of censorship prophesy will come the moment the "censors" take over. As a matter of fact, this anticipation of conformity under censorship is largely a bugaboo with which to frighten the unthinking. In ages when censorship did operate more stringently than at present, there was little conformity to be discerned.

Even in the period following the Council of Trent, "when the Church became a mighty patron of the arts, strictly controlling them as a means toward edification and devotion, the range of personal expression among artists was remarkable; so that painters such as Annibale Carracci and Caravaggio could flourish at the same time. The same holds true even among the portrait painters. Working amidst the rigid ceremonial of the Spanish Court, Velasquez and Goya could produce portraits conforming to every regulation for official work, but make them devastating revelations of the individuals concerned. The examples quoted have all been taken from painting; but the same holds good for sculpture, music and literature."[1]

As in the past, so in the present. The censorship (control) activities under Catholic auspices which we shall examine in the second part of this book embody small threat indeed of imposing on the artist (the writer or the film producer) a dead uniformity that would spring from a timidity to experiment lest he would find himself running afoul of the "censors." As a matter of historical fact, it was immediately after the inauguration of the Legion of Decency, and as a direct result of the Legion's demand for moral improvement, that the motion-picture industry rose to new heights of artistic film-making. There is significance in the fact, too, that since the Legion began screening films in 1936, not a single picture that has won an Oscar has been a C (condemned) film; only seven have been rated B (morally objectionable in part for all). In other words, since 1936, fourteen of the twenty-one Oscar-winning films have been either A-1 or A-2. It is indeed hard to see how the Legion's activities have laid a dead hand of cultural conformity on the imagination of Hollywood.

In all seriousness, the conformity we have to fear in our American society is the trend toward "letting the government do it." And an approach to such an attitude is in the making when groups like the American Civil Liberties Union try to control (censor) the efforts of other groups like the Legion

---

[1] William G. Constable, "Problems of Freedom and Authority in the Arts," in *Freedom and Authority in Our Time* (The Twelfth Symposium of the Conference on Science, Philosophy and Religion), edited by Lyman Bryson and others (New York: Harper, 1953), p. 379.

and the National Office for Decent Literature (NODL) to control (censor). This statement gets us, of course, exactly nowhere; it results in the boring round-and-round-the-mulberry-bush routine of repeating, "You have no right to censor my right to censor." But I submit that if the Legion and the NODL ever get put out of business—as seems the goal the anti-censorship bodies have in mind—then the American cultural scene will be the poorer, because two vigorously protesting voices will have been stilled, and art has always flourished when it has had to meet the challenge of protest against some of its vagaries.

A puzzle immediately faces one when trying to find out just what the opponents of censorship mean. Statement after statement, as will become evident in the body of this work, claims that *any* censorship is useless, because impractical; and dangerous, because in violation of our democratic traditions and practices. Censorship, one would accordingly conclude, is a bad thing, and the sooner we sweep away all forms of it the better. But at the same time, the anti-censorship groups proclaim as a prelude to their arguments that they, too, are strongly opposed to pornography, obscenity in literature and the arts. If so (and we take them at their word), then they are *ipso facto* in favor of at least the minimum censorship necessary to keep such stuff to a minimum availability. In other words, the anti-censors know what anyone realizes who gives the subject a moment's thought; namely, that in any civilized society *some* forms of censorship are simply inherent in the fact that people live together. But their manifestos softpedal such a realization, and one cannot help feeling that, despite their stated distaste for obscenity, theirs is a laissez-faire philosophy which would allow *anything* in literature and the arts absolutely free circulation, with society helpless to do a thing except through strictly legal means.

But law is not the only means at hand for society to use for the protection of the common good. Social forces such as custom and tradition are at work constantly, shaping and forming our democratic life—traditions and customs that may be somewhat opposed to one another, but which, existing in an atmosphere of free debate, enrich our cultural lives. The law may, indeed, have to be called upon or step in of its own accord to settle this or that dispute. The law may be and frequently is the final arbiter, but it is not always the first court of appeal.

This leads to the second puzzle about the anti-censorship forces. Believing that strictly legal process is the only proper source for the control (censorship?) of books and films, they are driven to the point of practically accusing any extra-legal operations of being *anti*-legal. This is evident in the way in which they employ such words as "pressure," "boycott," "picketing." To be sure, statements of the ACLU (to take this very active organization as an example) do admit, if one reads them carefully, that boycott, for instance, is not necessarily illegal. But in press releases and in the general furor that is stirred up by a particular instance of censorship, "boycott" and "economic pressure" are bandied about in such fashion that the cursory reader is bound to get the impression that such methods of operation fly in the face of the law. This, as I shall try to develop later, is a "scare" tactic that proves more divisive, in my opinion, than the activities of the various "censorship" groups.

A further demarcation of the subject matter of this book seems necessary. We are here dealing only with censorship in cultural matters; we shall have nothing to say about political censorship. Whether or not the FBI files should be kept secret or opened to defense counsels does not concern us here. And, to be still more specific, we shall treat censorship only in the matter of printed material (books, pocket-size books, magazines, comics, etc.) and motion pictures. These are the two fields that are currently most embroiled in the problem of cultural censorship, and to make the treatment concrete, we shall confine ourselves to the activities of the National Legion of Decency and the National Office for Decent Literature, the most prominent and active organs of "Catholic censorship."

In this framework, then, the question to be treated is this: Is there anything like an official stand of the Catholic Church on the matter of censorship? Yes, there is. This position springs from some fundamental philosophy and from some positive ecclesiastical law. It can be found in the Code of Canon Law and in the authoritative commentaries on the

Code. It is a position, needless to say, that directly affects Catholics only, for whom the law is made. It is, further, a position that does not rest merely on a statement of general principles; it descends to fairly detailed practice. This is *the* Catholic viewpoint.

When we leave this fairly restricted field and examine the *operations* of censorship as engaged in by some Catholic agencies, we can no longer state that we are expounding *the* Catholic viewpoint. The principles on which the Legion and the NODL are based are certainly Catholic principles which are stated in Canon Law. But on the actual operation of these two bodies there is not unanimous Catholic consensus. Not every Catholic, loyal to the Legion principles though he may be, agrees on the B rating, let us say, given to a particular film. Not every Catholic thinks that the NODL is alert enough, to take another example, in disowning some types of use to which its list of disapproved books is put.

The Catholic viewpoint about particular operations of Catholic censorship outside of that envisioned in the Code of Canon Law is that *there are several possible and legitimate viewpoints.* If this fact alone comes to the appreciation of those who so vigorously oppose the Legion and the NODL, this book will have been of some small service, for it will have revealed that the Church is not quite so monolithic, so "regimented" as many souls think.

One final word. This book is not, in its author's mind, a debater's handbook. I hope that there is no note of simple attack and rebuttal in it. To be sure, charges leveled against the Legion and the NODL will have to be handled, but the purpose of it all is not to reduce opponents to silence. If the ACLU, the American Book Publishers Council, the Authors League, and others disagree with the Legion and the NODL, by all means let them continue to say so. But perhaps if they realize somewhat more clearly the spirit of *the* Catholic viewpoint on censorship, they may more temperately assess the goals and operations of Catholic agencies at work in our pluralistic society.

That is the only hope I have in this book: not that discussion will be stilled, but that further discussion may proceed with more reasonableness and intelligent responsibility on both sides—those who are against all censorship in both principle and practice, and those who are for it in principle and trying to work it out in practice in full accord with our American principles of freedom.

PART I

THE POSITION OF THE CHURCH

CHAPTER I

Authority and the Role of Coercion

It may seem like taking a very long running start indeed in order to essay a modest broad jump, but any discussion of the problems of modern, and especially American, censorship cannot be sensibly undertaken without laying first a basis for argumentation by sketching the Catholic philosophy on the state and on human freedom. It is to be hoped that the term "Catholic philosophy" will not annoy those not of the Catholic faith who may chance to read these words. The phrase is not used in the sense of describing a "sectarian" system of thought. The philosophy referred to is indeed more aptly termed the *philosophia perennis*, for its roots lie far back in the Judaic and Greco-Roman world, were developed by the medieval Christian philosophers, and have borne fruit in the thinking of the framers of our Declaration of Independence. Many philosophers, political scientists, thinkers on the problems of government and the relations of Church and state hold, at least in general outline, the philosophy of the state and of human freedom that will be sketched in this and the following chapter.

To begin at the beginning, this philosophy holds that the state is a "natural" institution. This means that man, by his very nature, spontaneously but inevitably forms a community with his fellow men; that man is, of his very nature, a "social" being. Since man's nature comes from God, and since man's impulses toward communal living are a natural consequence of his being man, this gravitation is also God-given. This is seen most obviously in the institution of marriage. The first society to which man is naturally drawn, both by the exigencies of his nature and by his historical development, is the familial society. This seminal society, however, proves itself to be inadequate for the fulfillment of man's deepest desires and needs, and so man is induced again by the very bent of his nature to associate with other families—for mutual sociability, protection, comfort, development, and so on.

But, together with his impulses toward societal living, man, even in society, still possesses his individual will, his particular desires and ambitions. Given this fact, itself another God-given attribute, society is faced immediately with the problem of a number of individuals and families trying to get along together for some common purpose, toward some mutually agreed goal—protection against outside inimical forces, let us say, or the development of agricultural ways and means. Obviously there arises the necessity of some compromise; individual differences must be resolved; somebody, or some group selected to deliberate and speak for the whole community, has to make the decisions. And so arises, just as naturally and just as clearly God-given in origin as man's societal nature itself, the institution of authority.

It is not to be thought that authority in a community takes its origin from deficiency. The necessity of authority does not spring from sin—as though only in a group of fallible and fumbling human beings is authority a necessity. Far from being a necessary evil, authority results from the very perfection of the human beings it is destined to weld into community life. Authority arises from the fact of each individual's free will: it is because each one has free will that individuality must be harnessed, so to speak, if the individuals are to pull as a team for the cohesion and advancement of the community.

Authority in a community, then, has more than what is called a "substitutional" function—that is, a function that makes up for some inherent deficiency in the body to be governed. To be sure, some of the obvious instances of authority that spring to mind show us authority being exercised because there is some sort of "deficiency" in those governed. So parents, for example, exercise their authority over minor children because the children cannot yet know what is best for them. But even if children became overnight as wise and kind and prudent as their parents, parental authority would still exist (though its open exercise might be minimized) because of the very fact that common action in the family demands a source from which decisions must come.

Now the reason for this rather long disquisition on a fundamental concept, which most men of good will find no difficulty in accepting, is that a consequence that is largely overlooked may be brought to light. The consequence is simply and, perhaps to some, startlingly this: authority is not only to be respected but *loved*. If the common purpose of a family—mutual love, peace, prosperity, and so on—is a purpose worthy of love, then the authority that directs the family to that purpose is worthy of love, and not only because authority is the human instrument through which the common purpose may be achieved, but because, just as the family and its essential purposes are natural (i.e., God-instituted), so the authority is natural (i.e., God-instituted).

This is true not merely from a consideration of the origin of society and of the authority which is necessary for the very existence of society, but from a consideration of the purpose or end for which society exists. That end or purpose, in general, is the common good, the good of society as a whole as distinguished from the good of the individuals who make up the whole. Individuals dwell in familial society in such fashion that desires, ambitions, modes of action that might be most delectable for the individual are forgone, sacrificed (or sublimated, as the current phrase goes) for the sake of the good of the whole family. Mother's craving for the mink coat or father's passion for golf yields—or should—to the needs of the family for decent prosperity. Individuals and families dwelling in civil society also conspire, or should conspire, to a common end, which we call the common good and which can be summed up in the phrase "peace and prosperity." An individual or a family yields to some extent its dominion over its wealth and property through the machinery of taxes, for example, not because they like to, but because it is for the common good.

Authority, therefore, is to be respected and loved, not only because it comes, reductively, as the philosophers would say, from God, but because, in its legitimate exercise, it also leads (reductively) to God, because such exercise of authority leads to the common good which is also willed by God.

This philosophy of authority is not only down-to-earth, it reaches to heaven in its sublimity. It may sound like the veriest idealism, but it is not for that reason utopian. Common sense alone will tell us that, if authority is not loved, the vagaries to which any exercise of human authority is subject will sooner or later bring that authority to be feared or hated. It is perhaps almost inevitable, because of the earthiness of our human emotions, that a neutral and sort of bloodless respect for authority cannot long hold the field. This is especially true since authority is not infrequently vested in a person or a party one feels he cannot validly respect. In such a case, if the *principle* of authority is not loved, its imposition by one who is not respected comes easily to bring law and order under fear, suspicion, and hatred. Then one will obey because he must, not because he loves the common good which is, of itself, as the goal of societal action, lovable.

As has been hinted above, it does not follow from this line of thought that any and every *enactment* of authority must be loved. Some enactments may be onerous (such as the paying of taxes) but just; in this case the enactment must be respected, not only in thought, but in actual fulfillment. Other enactments may be ill-considered (such as our late Prohibition law) or unjust; in this case there is recourse, in a properly constituted state, to redress. So we have the system of constitutional checks and balances by which the enactments of the legislative arm are subject to review by the judiciary; thus the goal of the common good, though lost sight of for a time, may be restored as the only proper purpose of the state.

But the principle remains unshaken. Authority, as the necessary instrument by which the parts of the societal whole may conspire to a common end, is an object of love.

The particular relevance of this principle to the problem of censorship will become clear, it is to be hoped, throughout the whole course of this book. Its particular relevance here depends on another aspect of law and authority which must now fit into this preliminary chapter.

One of the essential postulates of law is authority's coercive power. If a society is to strive with any hope of success toward a common goal—peace and prosperity in a commonwealth— the authority governing that society must not only be able to pass laws and to reassess those laws constantly as circumstances change (the role of the interpretations of our Supreme Court);

it must also be enabled to enforce those laws and to exact penalties for their violation. This is obviously the point at which respect for authority, let alone love for it, as we have been considering above, comes in for its severest test. It is one thing to be all in favor of sane traffic laws and even to love them in a theoretical sort of way while you are snug in your armchair or gleefully watching some road hog getting his comeuppance at the hands of a traffic cop. It is quite another thing to love the authority that slaps a ticket on you because you temporarily forgot your respect for (and love of) the law. Coercion is never pleasant for those being coerced and, quite obviously, coercion can overstep proper bounds and turn into injustice and tyranny. But coercion that is exercised as a means to prevent the frustration of the common good is as worthy of respect and love as is the authority it is designed to uphold.

One consideration that may serve to put the coercive aspect of law and authority into proper perspective is a consideration of the educative or pedagogical quality of coercion. Restrictions merely for the sake of restriction are never proper or valid, either morally or politically. Such restrictions would be purely the result of the whim of the authority—or, worse, of malice. Restrictions are valid only if they are for the sake of a greater good, a greater liberty. To be restrained to drive your car at not more than fifty miles an hour is an improper infringement of your liberty, *unless* that very restriction allows drivers in general (and pedestrians) a reasonably assured freedom from danger to life and limb.

This principle is so valid that not even the restrictions which God's law puts on our human actions are good *merely* because they are restrictions. The negative precepts of the Ten Commandments look always to a positive freedom. "Thou shalt not commit adultery" means that if you avoid this threat to the stability, happiness, and holiness of married union you will be freed from a burden so that you may go on from there to the fullness of married life as God intends it. The negative precepts, accordingly, may be looked upon as simply clearing away the roadblocks thrown up by our pride and sensuality so that the greater freedom may operate, and that freedom is positive and glorious: "You shall *love* God with your whole heart and with your whole soul and with all your mind, and your neighbor as yourself," or, more gloriously still, "as Christ has loved you."

If the coercive aspect of law and authority is looked on in this way, as a means toward a greater freedom, the pedagogical aspect of coercion becomes clear. Coercion by way of consequence instructs the members of a society (family or state), although the instruction may be painful, that there *is* a common good which the offending member may have been habitually ignoring or temporarily forgetting. St. Thomas Aquinas has much to say on this matter of the pedagogical value of coercion, especially in his *Summa Theologica* (1a–2ae, 95, 1). Here, for instance, is one commentary on the teaching of the Saint:

"Every man needs education and virtuous training. Paternal training, whose proper instrument is persuasion, provides sufficiently for the training of youths who are prone to virtue; on the contrary, those who are prone to vice must be prevented by coercion from doing wrong. . . . By compelling bad boys from doing wrong, a twofold result is secured: first, the tranquillity of honest people is assured; secondly, the bad boys themselves get used to acting honestly, so that they may finally become virtuous, having become able to do voluntarily what they previously did by fear of punishment.

"This elevated conception of the pedagogical function of coercion rests upon the psychological fact that a good habit generated by fear, although non-virtuous in its origin, makes virtue easier, the substitution of good will for fear taking place easily when the exterior acts of virtue have become habitual. Coercion, in the long run, paves the way for persuasion, because habitual automatism turns to voluntariness."[1]

The skeptic or the cynic will probably retort that this concept of the pedagogical value of coercion is a pipe dream and that it is extremely doubtful that the wrongdoer is ever so persuaded by force and restraint that he comes to will and love the good. This happy result is certainly to be discerned frequently enough in the sanctuary of conscience: the sinner,

[1] Yves Simon, *Nature and Functions of Authority* (Milwaukee: Marquette University Press, 1940), p. 54.

restrained by the fear of hell, for instance, can and does come to love the good. But the point of this discussion is quite other. It may be that in the sphere of external activity—in civic, social, and political life—the mere fact of restraint or coercion rarely convinces the wrongdoer of the good to be desired. It may be that the extortionist or the blackmailer or the arsonist, clapped into jail to restrain his felonous acts, is simply biding his time and meditating ways and means to resume his ill-advised manner of life.

But those who are not so coerced, those who are concerned with the problems of respect for law and authority—they are the ones who ought to be able to consider with dispassion this whole matter of the coercive aspect of authority. The sorry fact of the matter is, however, that all too frequently the very ones who ought to be concerned with the very highest and most exalted concepts of the law are often the ones who, perhaps all unwittingly, are whittling away at one of the very foundations of respect for law—the foundation of its coercive power. So, in this matter of censorship, protests by such organizations as the American Civil Liberties Union against any and all exercises of "censorship" all too often sound as though they are based on the assumption that all coercion exercised by authority is a bad and evil thing, both in itself and in its consequences. Thus, for instance, the following statement issued by the Authors League of America (as reported in the New York *Times* for May 9, 1957):

"[The League has noted] with increasing concern, in the decade since the Second World War, a drift in our national life toward censorship. . . . The impetus in this authoritarian drift is coming mainly from groups who above all should hold totalitarianism in abhorrence: a few religious organizations and a few patriotic organizations, where zeal has overcome wisdom . . .

"The Authors League denies the right of any individual or group in the United States to set limits on the freedom to write, which includes the freedom of publication, distribution and performance of writings."

The obvious drift of this statement, of course, is directed toward groups which endeavor to "censor" outside the operation of the law; but two overtones, it is to be suspected, are also evident. The first is that "censorship" is *ipso facto* "totalitarian." This is a point to be proved, not merely asserted. Beyond that seems to lie the confusion against which this whole chapter is directed: namely, that all coercion or restraint imposed by society on the individual is wrong.

This consideration, however, needs further development in the following chapter, in which we shall discuss more fully the problem of human freedom in the face of legitimate authority. Underlying the false estimate of coercion as being merely a negating and restrictive aspect of authority is the equally false assumption that whatever, especially in a democracy, curtails freedom (but what *type* of freedom is rarely defined, though here lies the specific problem) impedes "progress." The Catholic concept, on the other hand, holds that the very idea of human progress implies necessarily the correlative idea of measure and restraint, internally in a man's own conscience and motives, and externally through the operation of law and of social forces which are not formally legal.

The suspicion that the coercive aspects of authority and law are not to be tolerated by free men is a holdover from the philosophic liberalism of the nineteenth century. The most familiar expression of this bent of mind is found in the cant expression that "ideas have to make their way in the market place." Perhaps the most cogent phrasing of this philosophy is found in the following passage:

"If we refrain from coercing a man for his own good, it is not because his good is indifferent to us, but because it cannot be furthered by coercion. The difficulty is founded on the nature of the good, itself, which on its personal side depends on the spontaneous flow of feeling checked and guided not by external restraint, but by rational self-control. To try to form character by coercion is to destroy it in the making. Personality is not built up from without but grows from within, and the function of the outer order is not to create it, but to provide for it the most suitable conditions for growth. Thus, to the common question whether it is possible to make men good by Act of Parliament, the reply is that it is not possible to compel morality because morality is the act or character of a free agent, but that it is possible to create the conditions under which morality can develop, and among these not the least important is freedom from compulsion by others."[2]

Commenting on this statement, Yves Simon pithily remarks: "The point is, precisely, that good habits possibly determined by coercion are to be numbered among these 'conditions under which morality can develop.'"[3]

Again, these liberals and their modern progeny claim that "an absolute freedom of thought and expression [is] justified, their idea being that in any circumstances whatever, truth can but profit by unrestricted freedom."[4] Let truth go out and jostle with error in the market place, they proclaim, do not restrain or limit error and the expression of it, and the truth will always win out. Now, certainly the Catholic position entertains the utmost respect for the power of truth (*magna est veritas et praevalebit*) and for its ultimate triumph, but that respect is not so naïve as to believe that here and now, in these circumstances, when the truth should already have won and its delayed victory imperils the common good, error must be left uncontrolled. Professor Simon puts his finger on this liberal philosophical error when he says:

"The contribution of error to the development of truth is but a happy occurrence, whose regularity is not guaranteed by any steady principle. Liberals ascribe to accidental occurrences a regularity that accident does not admit of. At the *heart of Liberalism* lies an almost religious belief in a kind of Demiurge immanent in the stream of contingent events, or better, identical with the very stream of contingencies. . . . Owing to this benevolent Spirit of Nature, contingency and chance are supposed to result indefectibly in happy achievements. Wrong use of the human freedom, in the long run at least, does not matter. Regarding both truth-values and economic values, the Liberal confidently relies upon the *laissez faire laissez passer* system. Liberalism is an *optimistic naturalism*."[5]

Another aspect of the "optimistic naturalism" of philosophic liberalism is the rather naïve idolatry of the power of mere education, and by that is meant any educative process

[2] L. T. Hobhouse, *Liberalism* (New York: Holt, 1911), p. 143.
[3] *Op. cit.*, p. 56.
[4] *Ibid.*, p. 59.
[5] *Ibid.*, pp. 61–62.

that insists exclusively on the freedom to examine and learn. With reference to the problem of censorship, the argument would run that if only "good" books, movies, and what not were made increasingly widespread for the consuming public they would inevitably drive out the "bad." This stand is based, as will be evident, on the prior assumption that the truth will always vanquish error if allowed to compete on an equal footing. But any "equal footing" rests on the further assumption that all men are equal in taste, inclination to virtue, powers of self-control, and a host of other qualities. Surely it is a fact of experience, which even the foes of all and every censorship are themselves constrained to admit, that some people who have indeed been exposed to "good" literature throughout many years of education still seem to prefer the "art" and "girlie" magazines to the reasonably priced classics that can be found on the very same newsstands.

This is not to underestimate the power of education but simply to restate that the educative process, no less than the process of law, necessarily entails a restrictive or coercive element. If the goal of education is a glorious and positive "do" —*do* grow into the full stature of integral manhood—it can be reached only by some inculcation of many a "don't"—*don't* dissipate your energies, debauch your potentialities by running after goals that are unworthy of a man. C. S. Lewis, in his thoughtful and challenging little book, *The Abolition of Man*, has much to say on this entire subject. Here is a small passage which underlines the thought that education alone is not enough to make a man virtuous:

"It still remains true that no justification of virtue will enable a man to be virtuous. Without the aid of *trained* [emphasis supplied] emotions, the intellect is powerless against the animal organism. I had sooner play cards with a man who was quite sceptical about ethics, but bred to believe that 'a gentleman does not cheat,' than against an irreproachable moral philosopher who had been brought up among sharpers. In battle it is not syllogisms that will keep the reluctant nerves and muscles to their post in the third hour of the bombardment."[6]

[6] C. S. Lewis, *The Abolition of Man* (New York: Macmillan, 1947), p. 15.

But the training of the emotions, of the will, of just and noble sentiments, what Plato calls the "spirited element," is something that implicates all sorts of restraining elements in education. The young trainee cannot be thrown out, naked and unarmed, into the market place of clashing ideas and expected to see at once—or perhaps ever—the beauty and force of the truth. Mere exposure to "facts" will never add up to human education. As Mr. Lewis remarks of one he calls the "Innovator" (he is the holder of the thesis that man will always obey the truth if exposed to it): "[He] is trying to get a conclusion in the imperative mood out of premises in the indicative mood; and though he continues trying to all eternity he cannot succeed, for the thing is impossible."[7] To put the potential reader, for instance, in the presence of "good" and "bad" literature, before an openly pornographic book and a wholesome one, and say, "See, the one is good and the other bad," will never, of itself, induce in the reader the conclusion, "I ought to read the one and avoid the other." The premises for that conclusion have to come from a deeper source than the mere struggle between truth and error in the market place. Part of the source is the restrictive or coercive aspect of both law and education.

This stage of our discussion leads immediately into the thorny problem of the proper balance between law (and education) and human freedom. Before we go on to that, however, let us try to gather together some conclusions.

The Catholic viewpoint is that law is to be loved because it is rational and because of its origin and purpose. Its origin is from God; its ultimate purpose is rationally to assure a just freedom.

One of the necessary postulates of law (or of the exercise of law through authority) is the community's coercive power, the restriction and punishment of evil-doing, of infringements of the law. This onerous element is not less to be loved than the expansive aspects, for it is destined for the same purpose, to facilitate the exercise of freedom.

It follows, therefore, that society, which has the right and duty to establish laws for the common good, has, by the same

7 *Ibid.*, p. 20.

title, the right *and the duty* to exercise coercion. It would seem superfluous to emphasize this truth were it not for the fact that most of the controversy about censorship seems to rest fundamentally at exactly this crux. A great number of those who oppose censorship in any shape or form deny implicitly (though they may never advert to the fact) that society has the *right* to censor—especially the state in a pluralistic society like the one in which we live. We aver in these pages that the state not only has the *right* but is solemnly bound by the *duty* to censor, under certain circumstances.

It seems odd that this can apparently be the stand of opponents of censorship, since they are quite ready to admit other coercive powers of the state. No one of them would question the right of the state to arrest traffic-law violators, for instance, or to throw dope peddlers into jail, but when it comes to any restrictions or controls in the matter of freedom of expression, they will not only deny the state's duty to protect the common good, but will even call into question its right.

It is hard, no doubt, to reconcile the divergent statements of such organizations as the American Civil Liberties Union. In the "Statement on Censorship Activity by Private Organizations and the National Office of Decent Literature," issued to the press in May 1957, for instance, we read, on the one hand: "Since *any kind* [emphasis supplied] of censorship infringes that constitutionally guaranteed freedom of the press which protects the free exchange of ideas in our country, it is imperative that the American people be warned of the danger in which their freedom stands." Again: "The First and Fourteenth Amendments to the United States Constitution, and the constitutions of the several States, prohibit governmental abridgment of freedom of the press. If one may read, one must be able to buy; if one may buy, others must be able to print and sell." But on the other hand, the American Civil Liberties Union is constrained to recognize that the phrase, "any kind of censorship," is far too wide, for it goes on to state: "If curbs are to be placed on freedom of the press, and these curbs must be based on a clear and present danger of a substantive harm from the publication, they can be imposed only by our courts, through full legal process."

If the Constitution prohibits governmental abridgment of freedom of the press, how can the courts be exercising "full legal process" when they impose curbs, even under "clear and present danger"?

I do not see how the Union can have it both ways, and I believe their fundamental drive is to abolish all kinds of control on all possible kinds of expression and that their stand is that the "full legal process" under which the courts now act is itself unconstitutional. And this, if I am not reading too sinister a purpose into the convictions of men of good will, springs, it seems incontrovertible to me, from a false concept of the nature of coercion in the authority of government.

A further example. In *The Freedom to Read*, published for the National Book Committee, the authors state: "We have argued on philosophic grounds [we shall advert to these arguments in our next chapter] that censorship is unsound, impractical and undesirable." Yet in the very next sentence they go on to say: "On political grounds, recognizing that censorship in the broad sense has been and is being practiced, we shall consider how its operation can be kept strictly in conformity with law and the preservation of rights, in order that it shall not impede directly or indirectly the freedom of expression by which, among other consequences, the dangers of censorship may become more generally recognized."[8] But, again, here is an inconsistency. If censorship is indeed "unsound, impractical and undesirable," then any "law" dealing with it ought to be concerned wholly and solely with eliminating it, lock, stock, and barrel.

The thought will not die that we are back at a basic misapprehension—that any restriction of "freedom" is a block to "progress," and hence that any coercive aspects of the law are always, by their nature, bad aspects and should therefore not only be held to a minimum, which all admit, but eliminated altogether.

Inevitably we come at this point to a consideration of "freedom." Is it an absolute? What is it? Is it the only and essentially indispensable atmosphere under which "progress" can flourish? Before we essay some thoughts on this and, ob-

8 By Richard McKeon, Robert K. Merton, and Walter Gellhorn (New York: R. R. Bowker Co., 1957), p. 11.

viously, on its connection with the problems of censorship, let us close this chapter with a pertinent thought from St. Thomas:

"Laws are passed to ensure the smooth running of the commonwealth. Unrestricted rights are not allowed in any civil constitution. Even in a democratic state, where the whole people exercise power, rights are not absolute but relative, though from the equal liberty of all subjects under the law the state may be described as predominantly equalitarian. The statutes passed by a democracy may be just, not because they reach pure and perfect justice, but because they fit the purpose of the regime."[9]

Perhaps, after all is said and done, the opponents of all and any censorship, who are, it would seem, the proponents of freedom as an absolute, are devoted to a false ideal of law which does not take sufficiently into account the fact that law, as we know it, is for poor, fallible, striving human beings who *need* the pedagogy of coercion and restraint no less than the expansive skies of liberty and freedom.

CHAPTER II

Freedom's Proper Limits

The Freedom to Read! This is something of a catch phrase and is brandished like an admonitory finger or a demolishing shillelagh against those who cannot bring themselves to think that anyone has the right to read anything at any time and place and under any circumstances whatever. The phrase is frequently used in connection with another glib and even meaningless "freedom"—"freedom of thought." The simple fact of the matter is that in one sense thought can be nothing

[9] Commentary in V *Ethics*, lect. 2. This and all subsequent quotations from St. Thomas are taken from the rich store to be found in *St. Thomas Aquinas: Philosophical Texts*, by Thomas Gilby (New York: Oxford Press, 1951), especially from the sections on "Law" and "Community and Society," pp. 352–93.

else than free. I can sit back and think about what I like and
no power in God's world can prevent me. Even attempts at
brainwashing, physical torture, moral pressure—none of these
can deprive me of the power to think what I want here and
now to think about. This seems pretty obvious; but when
"freedom of thought" is linked with "freedom of expression"
or "freedom to read," the picture begins to get confused, for
thought, in so far as it is the internal working of my own
mind, is a purely private thing, as private as the stirrings of
my conscience. But as soon as we add the notion of the *expression* of thought—in speech, in the printed or broadcast or
televised word—we are in a different domain. We are in the
domain of social influences and consequences. And it is at least
theoretically possible, is it not? that the thought I am "free"
to entertain in the sanctuary of my own consciousness is a
thought that I may not be "free" to express in public. A
chemistry teacher is free to think, if he gets any fun out of the
process, that water is composed of gin and putty, but he is
not free to teach that to his eager pupils. No one can pre-
censor him the moment before he utters this ingenious theory
before his class, but he most certainly will be "censored"
post factum and told in firm terms not to teach this quaint
doctrine again—or else find himself a position on the faculty
of a school in Never-Never Land.

This may be a silly example, but perhaps it will serve to
indicate how the concept of freedom gets bandied about in
discussion, especially in debates on the problems of censorship. I should like in this chapter to try to disentangle some of
the ideas on freedom, and I shall take as my point of departure
some of the statements that appear in the recently published
The Freedom to Read, a book referred to earlier. I take this
as a jumping-off point because the book is the fruit of much
thought, apparently, and represents the efforts of what is perhaps the most scholarly approach to date by those who are
stern-faced against censorship. May I repeat what I said in
the Introduction, however, that I am not attempting to refute.
I am interested only in trying to state with precision what the
Catholic position is—and here, specifically, the Catholic position on the matter of human freedom and its correlation with
human authority. Quite apart from the matter of censorship,

this correlation, its possibility, its limitations, its challenge, is probably the most crucial question in the ideological quiz program in which we are all, willy-nilly, these days engaged.

Censorship, states *The Freedom to Read*, is advocated on philosophical, moral, social, and/or political principles. The philosophical principles, according to this book, and the arguments which are used to uphold them, however, do not cut much ice, for they have to be embodied in the particular society, many of whose members may not acknowledge the principles. In the Catholic view, however, it is of crucial importance to establish the rational philosophical principles, for if they *are* rational, then all men of good will can be led to accept them or, at the very least, to refuse amicably, if they feel they still must refuse, to see their rationality. This second alternative is probably the best that can be hoped for as a result of this essay.

There are two basic philosophies of freedom, begins *The Freedom to Read*:

"Freedom is conceived by some to consist in the ability to do as one pleases, whether or not one does as one ought; it is conceived by others to consist in the ability to do as one ought, whether or not one wishes to. Freedom may be defined in both views as 'absence of external constraint,' but external constraints are differently conceived according to different basic conceptions of man and the constraining influences that environ him."

Let us note here in passing that this position on the two attitudes toward freedom attributes to both attitudes a recognition that man is "environed" by some "constraining influences," among which we must, if we follow the thinking of our first chapter, include human law and authority. More on this point later, however. The book then goes on:

"The proponents of the second view hold that only the wise man is truly free, and therefore acts in accordance with his own nature; they argue that a man is not free when he acts under the influence of erroneous ideas or passions, since these are both the results of external circumstances. This view of freedom was expressed by Plato, the Stoics, St. Augustine, Spinoza, Hegel and Bergson, among others. The proponents of the first view hold that a man is free only if he acts in the light of his own preferences and decisions; they argue that he is constrained whenever he is limited to one possible course of action, even if the limitation is thought to be justified by someone else's decision concerning what is good and true. This view of freedom was expressed by Aristotle, Locke, Bentham, Mill, Dewey and Maritain, among others."[1]

Here we have run into a basic confusion, a failure to distinguish between a freedom of choice (the actual status of the will as a self-determining agent) and what has been called "terminal freedom" (the actual exercise of the free will of man as a social being).

But before we go on to clarify these two concepts of freedom, let us take this occasion to remark that no Catholic philosopher, nor any philosopher working in the tradition of the *philosophia perennis*, has ever held that freedom, adequately conceived, can be simply described as "the ability to act as one pleases." Let us see, for example, what Jacques Maritain says in this matter, and judge whether or not he is to be lumped with John Dewey.

"One may build social life on Freedom taken in the sense of *freedom of choice* and as an end in itself—a conception that one may call liberal or individual. . . .

"In this conception culture and society have for their essential office the preservation of something given: the free will of Man; in such a way that all possible acts of free choice may be available and that men may appear like so many little gods, with no other restriction on their freedom save that they are not to hinder a similar freedom on the part of their neighbor. Truth to tell, this political philosophy suffers from an unconscious form of hypocrisy, for it ignores for the benefit of man in the abstract all the heavy and severe burdens that lie on man in real life, the fact being that a limited number are enabled to enjoy this kind of Freedom only by oppression of the remainder of their fellows. The essential values of social justice and the common good are forgotten."[2]

Freedom has not been adequately defined when one stops at "freedom of choice." This innate freedom of the human will

[1] Pp. 2-3.
[2] Jacques Maritain, *Freedom in the Modern World* (London: Sheed and Ward, 1935), p. 40.

is a prerequisite to adequate freedom; it does not constitute
its essence:

"Freedom of choice is the *material* element in moral action
(and this includes social action, the mode of action of the
good citizen), since only free acts are capable of being regu-
lated by moral rules. . . . It is reason that gives form and
measure. An act is not of more value in morals because it
contains a greater measure of freedom; on the contrary, to act
for the mere pleasure of acting, *solely to exercise one's sense
of freedom, is apt to be a sign of moral debility* [this emphasis added] . . . It is *consonance with reason*, as St.
Thomas says, that is the *formal* constituent of moral action.
[Formal, we may explain, means what gives the peculiar and
essential character to a thing.]"[3]

This line of thought, which is the Catholic viewpoint,
clearly exculpates Mr. Maritain from the charge that he is of
the school that holds that freedom is adequately described by
saying it consists in the ability to "act as one pleases." It may
serve the further and more important purpose of showing that
the Catholic idea of adequate freedom is poorly expressed,
indeed, when "to do as one ought" is reduced to mean simply
that "those who are competent to recognize dangerous evil
and error should have the responsibility and power to prevent
or curtail their operation in the community, at least on the
young, the inexperienced, or the uneducated."[4]

This, we are warned, leads to a "real and grave danger."
The danger lies in the fact that "the competent," to whom will
be left the authority "to determine what may be said and what
must be avoided as dangerous to morality, security and the
common good," may come little by little to shift their ground.
From feeling that they have been given the power because
they actually *are* competent, they may come to conceive that
the mere possession of the power assures the competence and
consequently that the better *is* better simply because they
say so. The upshot, we are warned, is that freedom, interpreted
as doing what one ought, "can lead to the authoritarian state
and to a unique prescriptive morality."[5]

[3] *Ibid.*, pp. 32–33.
[4] *The Freedom to Read*, pp. 5, 6.
[5] *Ibid.*, p. 6.

These might well indeed be the consequences if this were an adequate presentation of the Catholic viewpoint on freedom. But such an interpretation is a travesty. The fundamental "oughtness" under which a man can alone act with full freedom is not an "oughtness" that is merely handed down by wise men, by courts or judges or counselors. It is an "oughtness" that is handed to man by the faculty of his reason. This is not merely Catholic doctrine; it is a datum of common sense and experience. If a man *knows* that the world is shaped something like a Florida orange, is he free to say that he knows it is as flat as an Aunt Jemima pancake? Why, yes; he is free, if he wants to use his free will in that fantastic fashion. But if he so uses his free will—not merely in joke, but in consistent fashion—would not common sense say that he is a slave to prejudice, whim, a warped sense of humor, a perverted desire to be different? In the face of a recognized fact, there is no intellectual freedom to deny that fact. But this is not slavery; it is freedom in truth, and the more and more a man knows the truth, in whatever field of knowledge, the freer he is for the simple reason that he is in deeper and deeper touch with reality. The wider the scope of reality a man can take within his intellectual, social, moral, and political life, the more does his power to be a man—in simpler words, his power *to love*—expand.

Again I quote Maritain. Other sources and authorities on the Catholic viewpoint could readily be adduced, but since Maritain has been used to establish a distorted interpretation, it seems good to let him act rather as a spokesman. Here are some passages that reveal his interpretation of the Catholic viewpoint of how the "oughtness" of action is "imposed" on man. It is definitely not "imposed" simply by those who happen to be "competent" because they have the power.

"The 'objective order that is imposed on man' is, in a general way, that of the nature of things with their respective laws (and first and foremost human nature) and the order of truth and of supernatural life: it flows from the Eternal Law which is the Wisdom of the Maker of all things. And it is imposed on man by being expressed in his reason and in his conscience through vital entry and incorporation in his imminent activities of knowing and willing. It is a vital act to adhere to that which is and to acknowledge by our mind and will an order that we did not create.

"The good man . . . has no contact with the bloody hand of the law; he knows only its kind eyes, for he fulfills the law not out of compulsion, but out of love and his own free will . . ."[6]

There is a sense in which we can legitimately say that this "objective order of things" is imposed on human action, not indeed by those who are "competent" simply because they have power, but by those who have power because they are "competent." But the fact that power, in some sense, ought to be possessed by those who are competent is itself part of the objective order of things. And, indeed, this is the way our American democracy works out. Those who govern us do so with the consent of the governed, manifest in the orderly process of democratic election. They are designated by us, the people, to exercise the power (which, in the Catholic view, comes from God); and the basis of the delegation rests on the supposition that they are competent. Not every man in the street knows the law, and so we elect judges. If we did not think a specific candidate had the qualification of competence, we presumably would not elect him.

This is but to say that even in a democracy there is a hierarchy of order. One who feels that this is un-American or undemocratic may test it in practice by trying to tell the traffic cop and His Honor that his ideas of traffic regulations are as good as theirs. Once such a hierarchy of order is established (by democratic processes, we suppose), then those who have the *legitimate* power can, indeed, "impose" on the community, to the extent to which their authority extends, what the community "ought" to do—not for the good of the "competent" ones, but for the good of the community.

But—and here is the crucial point—this imposition is not arbitrary. The classic definition of law, formulated with greatest precision by St. Thomas Aquinas, is: "an ordinance of reason made for the common good by the public personage who has charge of the community, and promulgated." Law is not a statement of arbitrary decrees; it is a statement of what it is

6 *Ibid.*, pp. 78–79.

reasonable for a man to do, not only with respect to his private life, but primarily with respect to the life of the community.

It is precisely because in any state, even in a democratic state, in which all are equal before the law, not all citizens are equipped, either by temperament, education, opportunity, or what not, to determine for themselves what the social "ought" is that those "competent" ones with the legitimately delegated power have not only the right but the duty to "impose" social "oughts" on the citizens. But let it be repeated, those "oughts" cannot be legitimately imposed unless they are comfortable to reason, to the objective order of things. This is clear in the intellectual order. A state would be acting outside the framework of law if it should decree, let us say, that schools had to teach the Jemima pancake hocus-pocus about the shape of the globe. In the light of the evidence at hand, the world *is* orange-shaped; that is the objective order of things, and a law decreeing that this reality had to be denied would be no law, for it would be flying in the face of reason. This is not too farfetched an example; governments have decreed, for instance, that the primacy of the state over the individual ought to be taught in schools. This is an intellectual falsehood (as well as being fraught with monstrous social and moral consequences) and, as such, cannot be the subject matter for law, a reasonable ordination.

It is, however, when we leave the intellectual field and get into the field of social, and especially moral, activity that the incontrovertible principle of the "objective order of things" runs into practical difficulties. *Is* there, many ask, any objective order in moral acts? Who can define precisely what is right, what wrong? Some people say they know, but others disagree in many instances. Since not every American can so define, is it not therefore true that when any authority steps in and says we *have* to act thus or so that authority is "imposing" its arbitrary will just because it happens to have power? This would seem to be the position of those who oppose any kind and all kinds of censorship. Their position seems to be that, since 160 million Americans could never be brought to agree that such-and-such a book is "obscene," no one, not even the "wise and good," are "competent" to make a practical judgment about this particular book.

But this, again, is to misinterpret the function of law. Law is a rule of reason, but of the *practical* reason. No lawgiver is gifted with supreme wisdom and infallibility, but he has to *act* (it is his right and duty) in given circumstances. Here are some of St. Thomas' thoughts on this aspect of the law:

"The practical reason deals with activities in singular and contingent situations. Unlike the theoretical reason, it does not determine necessary truths. Consequently, human laws cannot have the unerring quality of scientifically demonstrated conclusions. Not every rule need possess final infallibility and certainty; as much as is possible in its class is enough."[7] Again: "Laws are laid down for human acts dealing with singular and contingent matters which can have infinite variations. To make a rule to fit every case is impossible. Legislators have to attend to what happens in the majority of cases and should frame their laws accordingly."[8] And finally: "Now, since the law-maker must deal in general terms, because of the impossibility of comprehending all particular instances, and since his general ruling cannot square with every case, he takes what happens in the great majority of cases, well aware that his directive will fail in some instances. A zoologist says that the human hand has four fingers and a thumb, and yet he recognizes that a freak may display fewer or more."[9]

We are concerned, at this stage of the discussion, with disengaging some confused ideas of freedom. It appears that the fundamental confusion lies in the subtle shift from initial freedom (the existence in the individual of the power of free will) to terminal freedom (the action of the will, especially in a societal context). If we look only at the faculty of free will, then the will is not free unless it can do what it wills ("do what it pleases," the phrase runs). But if we shift our gaze and consider the circumstances under which the will makes its free decision, then we have to hold, states the Catholic position, that the will is only terminally free when it wills to act as it ought to act in order to do what befits human

[7] *Summa Theologica*, 1a–2ae, xci, 3 ad 3.
[8] *Ibid.*, cxx, 1.
[9] V *Ethics*, lect. 16.

nature and the society in which human nature functions. It is hard, indeed impossible, to see how any community could exist if freedom consisted not merely in the innate "ability" of everyone to "do as he pleased" but in the actual carrying into social operation of that principle of utter individualism.

Not only does this confusion about freedom lie at the heart of the argumentation of the authors of *The Freedom to Read*, but, strange to say, their concept of the law is impossibly perfectionist. If laws against "obscenity" in books have ever unfairly banned any book, I read them as implying, then there should be *no* laws against obscenity. If a definition of "obscenity" cannot be framed that will apply always and only to just that quality, then no book can be legally called obscene. This position is poles away from the realistic attitude of St. Thomas and the whole Catholic tradition, which, holding adamantly to the reasonableness of law, still admits that human law is fallible at times, tentative and groping, but always inspired by the supreme goal of the common good.

At the same time that an impossible perfectionism is demanded of the law, however, the very basis of the law is being undermined by the fact, often concealed in such argumentation, that the demanders of the impossible perfection are shifting their emphasis from a rule of law to a rule of men. John Milton, in his famous and often misapplied *Areopagitica*, is frequently quoted to confirm the impossibility of a sensible censorship because no men will ever be found capable of exercising it properly. "How shall the licensers themselves," asks Milton, "be confided in, unless we confer on them, or they assume themselves above all others in the land, the grace of infallibility and incorruptedness?"[10]

10 One of the set pieces always drawn from the hat when the dangers of censorship are spread before us is Milton's *Areopagitica*, his impassioned defense of freedom of the press. But, says Norman St. John-Stevas in *Obscenity and the Law* (New York: Macmillan, 1956), p. 194: "Nor is the inevitable quotation from Milton—out of its historical and literary context—of any practical utility in the social conditions of the present time." The author then goes to remark that "the following passage from the *Areopagitica* is not so often quoted: 'I mean not tolerated popery, and open superstition, which as it extirpates all religious and civil supremacies, so itself should be extirpate, provided first that all charitable and compas-

This is to confuse the issue. The point is not whether the judges (the censors) are themselves law-abiding, good, or prudent; the point is whether there are objective reasons for the law and whether the judges know and apply these reasons. It is perhaps not an exaggeration to say that this appeal to the personalities of the judges, the lawgivers, springs ultimately from an application in the political field of the early heresy of Donatism. The followers of Donatus (in the fourth and fifth centuries) held that the efficacy of the Christian sacraments depended on the personal worthiness of the one who administered them. If a holy priest baptized, the baptism was not only valid, it was infused with "virtue" from the sanctity of the baptizer. If a priest of so-so virtue baptized, the sacrament would be valid but not possessed of much "zing," if we may say so. But if the priest was leading an evil life, then the sacrament would be of no use at all. This was early condemned by the Church (it was "censored") for the obvious reason that such a doctrine would penalize the recipient of the sacraments for a fault not imputable to him. It is interesting how this dogmatic condemnation foreshadowed the teaching of political science that the reasonableness, the authority,

---

sionate means be used to win and regain the weak and the misled; that also which is impious or evil absolutely either against faith or manners no law can possibly permit, that intends not to unlaw itself. . . .' "

Another example of bland assumption arises in the use that is often made of "the spirit of Jefferson," as a condemnation of those who grant the principle of censorship. But Thomas Jefferson himself actually advocated censorship of a kind. Says Samuel Eliot Morison in *Freedom in Contemporary Society* (Boston: Little, Brown, 1956), pp. 116–17: "Jefferson was undoubtedly a great man, but also in some respects a great humbug. After founding a university [the University of Virginia] 'based on the illimitable freedom of the human mind,' he wished to have the teaching of history and government there controlled by party principles—those of his own party, of course. Fearing lest a 'Richmond lawyer' (meaning a Federalist like John Marshall) be appointed professor of government, he wrote: 'It is our duty to guard against the dissemination of such principles among our youth . . . by a previous prescription of the texts to be followed in their discourses.' . . . This attempt to exclude from a university the entire body of Federal and national literature . . . would be ludicrous if it were not so pitiful, as one more instance of the intolerance in practice by advocates of freedom in theory."

the majesty of the civil law do not depend on any personal qualities of lawgiver or law-enforcer. And we carry this basic truth over into our everyday lives (or ought to) when we say, for example, that we "salute the uniform, not the man."

Freedom adequately defined, then, is, in the Catholic view, only "freedom to act as I ought." And the oughtness comes not from any quality of goodness or wisdom in those who "tell" me what I ought to do but from the reasonableness of the law, which can be *applied* only by the judges—not "cooked up" by them and "imposed."

To return now to the two divisions of "freedom" as made by the authors of *The Freedom to Read*. Their position is that, under either of the freedoms, the one to act as I please or the other to act as I ought, censorship is wrong.

"We are convinced that the reasons against censorship derived from both conceptions of freedom are sound. The arguments for censorship, on the contrary, endanger both varieties of freedom. Censorship based . . . on the concept of freedom to do as you please places censorship in the hands of the wise and good, if they happen also to have secured power. But since the possession of power is in either case essential, there is no practical way to distinguish the considered judgment of officials who are wise and good from the arbitrary judgment of officials who are unwise and bad. Power tends to corrupt, in censorship as in other modes of its exercise . . . We are convinced that the reasons against censorship as a danger to both varieties of freedom are cogent."[11]

We may eliminate, I trust, in the above quote, the words "good" and "bad"; we are not Donatists in discussing the law. And the words "wise" and "unwise" can apply only to the context: officials who are competent in the law and its application. The "nine old men" of our Supreme Court may not be Solomons in all things, but we trust they are at least approximations of Solon.

But if one ignores the rhetoric in the above *Freedom to Read* statement, certainly it recalls the ingenious way the Chinaman in Lamb's famous essay discovered to roast a pig. If there is no way to distinguish the "wise" from the "unwise"

[11] *Op. cit.*, p. 8.

official in the matter of censorship, how is it possible to make the distinction in other fields in which the officials officially speak? Congress passes a tax law. Is every congressman a fiscal expert? Perhaps not, but he has the advice of experts. But those congressmen who oppose the law have *their* experts. Who is wise? If we have to wait for utter and infallible wisdom on the part of our lawgivers, we shall never move; democracy dies of expectancy, its longing eyes fixed on the distant horizon, over which will never stride the heroic figure of the perfect "wise" man.

We have not yet tackled the problem of the puzzles that censorship occasions and must try to solve. There *are* great problems, which this essay will never adequately dispose of. That is not really the purpose of the book. It purports to state, with tentative accuracy, the Catholic position—nothing more.

Thus far we have been considering some basic concepts: a concept of law and a concept of freedom. Our position is that those who flatly oppose any censorship most frequently do so on a basis of law and freedom that the Catholic view does not and cannot hold. The coercive aspects of the law are conceived as being *merely* restrictive. But, in the words of St. Thomas: "In this life there is no punishment for punishment's sake. The time of last judgment has not yet come. The value of human penalties is medicinal and in so far they promote public security or the cure of the criminal."[12] It follows that the state has not only the right, but the duty, of restricting acts that are inimical to its own well-being. Freedom of the press and of expression can, in circumstances, be as legitimately subject to restriction as any other freedom—that of assembly, for instance, in times of catastrophe or plague.

Second, utter opposition to censorship rests on the conception of freedom that defines it as freedom to do as one pleases. This is liberalism of a type that the Catholic view repudiates, as we have indicated above. Not only that; it is a theory of individualism that is at variance with the American way and our legal traditions. In his classic *Free Speech in the United States*, Zechariah Chafee, Jr., has this significant passage:

[12] *Summa,* 2–2ae, lxviii, 1.

"The true meaning of freedom of speech seems to be this. One of the most important purposes of society and government is the discovery and spread of truth on subjects of general concern. . . . Nevertheless, there are other purposes of government, such as order, the training of the young, protection against external aggression. Unlimited discussion sometimes interferes with these purposes, which must then be balanced against freedom of speech, but freedom of speech ought to weigh very heavily on the scale. . . .

"Or, to put the matter another way, it is useless to define free speech by talk about rights. . . . To find the boundary line in any right, we must get behind rules to human facts. In our problem, we must regard the desires and needs of the individual human who wants to speak and those of the great groups of human beings among whom he speaks. That is, in technical language, there are individual interests and social interests, which must be balanced against each other, if they conflict, in order to determine which interest shall be sacrificed under the circumstances . . . It must never be forgotten that the balancing cannot be properly done unless all the interests involved are adequately ascertained, and the great evil about all this talk about rights is that each side is so busy denying the other's claim to rights that it entirely overlooks the human desires and needs behind that claim."[13]

If the coercive power of the law is too narrowly interpreted and if freedom, whether to speak or read or do anything else in a society, is taken as an absolute right, then the great and imperative human desires and needs will be lost in the shuffle. One final remark, rather in the nature of an aside, to conclude this second somewhat introductory chapter to the problems of censorship. It has often seemed to me that, in their very commendable zeal to protect civil rights, such organizations as the American Civil Liberties Union and the National Book Committee have lost sight of the human desires and needs, or, to put it another way, let their passion for individual liberties obscure their concern for the common good, though that phrase is frequently treated with scant respect by them; it is, they feel, one of many "vague definitions." If we may judge

[13] In the chapter "Free Speech in the Constitution," pp. 31–32 (Cambridge: Harvard University, 1941).

from a recent poll, admittedly limited, the people of the United States are not too interested in the battle of the "rights" of censorship or of complete freedom of speech. But they do have desires and needs. In May of 1957 the Minneapolis *Sunday-Tribune* published the results of a state-wide questionnaire in which the key question read: "A community in Minnesota [West St. Paul] has adopted a movie censorship law, under which any movie needs official permission before it can be shown. Do you approve or disapprove of such a law?" An amazing 71 per cent of the answers approved, on such grounds that movies were "vulgar," "sexy," played up "kid gangster stuff," contained "immoral dialog and costuming." I am not saying this is very wise or informed citizenship; I am not saying that the Catholic view heartily approves precensorship; we shall touch on these matters later. But I am definitely saying that the "experts" who maintain that books do little harm to children, or that definite harm cannot be proved, do not echo the thoughts of the American citizenry. Any group of parents you talk to will say that *some* controls have to come somewhere, and not only in their own home, where all proper control obviously must start, but from the forces of society as well.

How society can best, democratically and harmoniously, exercise such controls is the burden of the rest of this book. We shall begin the study with an examination of one society, the Catholic Church, and see how it exercises control over its own members. Strange as it may seem to many, the conclusion that will emerge, we hope, is that the prudence, charity, respect for individual freedom and other qualities evident in the Church's legislation might well be a model for all official censoring bodies (the courts and so on) and must be a model for groups of Catholics who feel impelled to do something to meet this very human desire and need of keeping the printed word and the films under some control, especially as they are spread today before the young.

CHAPTER III

The Partnership of Law and Liberty

"The historical origin of the *Index Librorum Prohibitorum*," says *The Freedom to Read* (p. 41), "is unknown." Though the phrase may intend to refer to the beginnings of censorship by civil governments, the meaning most readers will take is that it is not known when the Catholic Church first started putting books on the Index. If that is the meaning the authors intended to be inferred, then we must deny quite firmly that the origins of the Roman Index are shrouded in the mists of obscurity. Unfortunately, however, the purposes and justification for the Church's restrictive legislation in the matter of books *are* shrouded in mystery. Some Catholics themselves, no doubt, are in the dark about the matter; much more do non-Catholics suspect that the Index of Forbidden Books hides some sinister intention of the Church to widen control over books in general and the publishing of anything not covered by an equally mysterious and sinister *imprimatur*. The purpose of this chapter is to sketch the reasons for and the justification of such legislation by the Catholic Church. The second part of the chapter will give a brief historical résumé of the history of the Index.

Let us hark back to the discussion in the first chapter. Restrictions imposed by law, we there said, are never justified unless they are imposed for the sake of a higher freedom. Catholics call the Church their Mother, and so she is. Often when a child is commanded to do something and wonderingly asks, "But why?" an impatient or harassed mother will snap, "Because I say so!" Child psychologists will probably and with probable truth say that this is not the best reason in the world for demanding obedience, but really it *is* the fundamental reason. The mother has authority and the child should obey for the basic reason that the command comes from legitimate authority. But as the child grows in reason and the mother grows in tact, better obedience will be obtained if the child knows that the command was dictated not merely by authority but by reasoned, temperate, prudent, and loving authority, and so mother will take time out once and again to explain the reasons that motivate her authority. So it is with our Mother, the Church, in all disciplinary regulations that restrict freedom. The child of the Church obeys (or should) *because* of the command. However, behind the authority of the command always lies the concern for a higher freedom, and the better and more clearly that freedom is recognized, the more fruitful will be the obedience to the command.

Let us start, then, in delineating the higher freedom behind the Church's restrictions on reading with a statement that may, at first blush, seem extremely "liberal."

All the disciplinary regulations of the Church, found in the various parts of the Canon Law, start with the presumption that the Catholic, though bound to hold Catholic dogma and the tenets of the moral code, is free in the living of his daily life. It can be put this way. The Code of Canon Law does not begin by saying: "Don't make a move unless the Church says yes." It does not start with the presumption that everything is forbidden to the Catholic unless it is specifically allowed. It rather starts with the presumption that everything is legally allowed unless forbidden specifically by law—and forbidden, as we shall see, for a higher good. In this presumption in favor of freedom, Canon Law parallels the civil law, which, to take an example from criminal procedure, presumes that a man is innocent until proved guilty, not that he is guilty until proved innocent.

This presumption in favor of freedom is written into the very text of Canon Law. Canon 19, which falls in the section of the Code that deals with rules of interpretation, says: "Laws which decree a penalty, or restrict the free exercise of one's rights . . . are subject to strict interpretation." "Strict interpretation" means "that these laws are not to be extended to other cases, but are to be interpreted literally according to the proper meaning of the words."[1]

As an example of laws which "restrict the free exercise of one's rights," are mentioned (appositely for our purpose) "laws which forbid the reading of certain books: consequently,

[1] Amleto Giovanni Cicognani, *Canon Law* (Westminster: Newman, 1934), p. 615.

restrictions forbidding the reading of books which expressly treat of obscene matters or which are subversive to faith must be interpreted strictly."[2] What a sane light such interpretation will shed on the matter of defining "obscenity" will be treated later. One does not, if he is animated by the Catholic view on the matter, go about accusing any and every vulgar book of being "obscene." To broaden the term "obscene" in such wise would be to violate the canonical rules for "strict interpretation."

This is the serene atmosphere the Church establishes at the very start of its code of Catholic discipline. It assures, as it were, the Catholic body that, though restrictions may be necessary for a common good and a higher freedom, it need never fear that its freedom will be trampled over roughshod. This, indeed, is not surprising, for human freedom is a gift from God and exists and has its majesty prior to any positive human law, civil or ecclesiastical.

But what are the reasons for the Church's restrictions (strictly interpreted though they be) in the matter of reading? Once the reasons are grasped, the higher freedom toward which they are intrinsically directed will become clear.

The Church is the divinely appointed carrier of Christ's revelation and of Christian morals. His revelation is enshrined in the dogmas of the Church; morals are summed up in the Ten Commandments as understood by Christian tradition. The Church is to hold, pass on, and defend the faith and morals of the Catholic body. To perform this task, she has been equipped by her Founder with all that is needed to make her a "perfect" society. This technical phrase does not mean that every member of the Church is a saint; it means that the society which the Church is has in its essential constitution all that it needs to preserve, propagate, and defend itself. It follows that the Church has a threefold authority: legislative, executive, and judicial. It can establish laws (always, mind, within its mandate of preserving faith, morals, and collective survival—for no other purpose); it can carry them into execution; it can judge their observation and punish transgressions against them. It will be noted that these are

[2] *Ibid.*, p. 617.

the same aspects of authority that the Church vindicates for the civil power. The state, too, on its level, is a "perfect" society. Hence, the Church, by reason of its divine mandate, has not only the right but the *duty* of safeguarding the faith and morals of its subjects. This it does through such positive legislation as demanding observance of Sundays and holy days of obligation, abstinence and fasting at certain times, and—what we are concerned with—the restriction, under certain definite circumstances, of specific books and certain types of reading matter.

The Catholic Church has never gone along with the profound-sounding but really vapid statement we hear these days in connection with the effects books have or can have on morals. In the attempt to show that censorship of any type is unneeded, the opponents of restriction of reading matter for the young often come up with the statement that "no book has ever seduced a girl." But many a book *has* seduced many a girl, and people more mature than girls as well. Minds have been swayed to truth *and* to falsehood through reading, and a mind lured into error is a mind seduced—a type of seduction that may well be more lamentable and more pernicious than physical seduction. Though it is not wise to go all the way with some who make horror, crime, and sex comic books the root of our juvenile delinquency, there can be no doubt that *some* specific horrible offenses by the young can be and have been traced even to a specific comic book. Case histories of this type can be found in the perhaps too-exaggerated indictment of the comics by Dr. Frederic Wertham in his *Seduction of the Innocent* (Rinehart, 1954). When the words of André Gide were placed on the Index in 1955, there was a great outcry in many quarters. But years before, one who apparently knew whereof he spoke, Paul Claudel, had said that every young man in France he ever met who had lost his faith had been sadly influenced by Gide. Happily, on the other hand, we need do no more than recall the experience of St. Augustine and the mysterious voice saying to him, *"Tolle, lege* [Take and read]"—an experience that started his conversion and gave the Western world one of its intellectual giants—to realize that books cannot only seduce minds but inspire them as well.

Indeed, it has always seemed to me that those who belittle the deleterious influence of books are defeating their own case. They seem to have a low opinion of the very printed word they are trying to save from destruction at the hands of censorship, for if books cannot "seduce" anyone, how can they inspire anyone—or are all books of equal insipidity? The Church at the very least pays books the compliment of thinking that they are—some of them, at any rate—of tremendous importance; it regards them as foes of Christian life worthy of a kind of respect, as one respects the strength of the caged tiger. If some books are not explosive enough to be viewed with alarm, it would seem to follow that no books are worthy to be viewed with interest.

So much by way of digression. To come back to the point: the Catholic Church does most firmly hold that some books can "seduce," that they are of grave danger to the faith and morals of the generality of the Catholic body. Holding that, she is compelled, by her own internal logic and constitution, to protect the faithful. (The state, too, as we have seen, is equally *impelled*, if and when a grave danger to the commonwealth arises.) Hence the Church may forbid a book on the grounds of danger to faith and morals, and she may do it in one of two ways. She may specify the particular book by title and author (this is done by "placing the book on the Index") or by indicating types or categories of reading under which unspecified books may fall (these categories are contained in Canon 1399).

The *Index Librorum Prohibitorum* (the latest edition appeared in 1948, with an appendix including books proscribed up to December 31, 1945) is a listing of some four thousand titles.[3] No one, of course, has ever figured out how many books have been printed since Gutenberg came up with his invention around 1400; over the centuries millions of titles have appeared. The point is that the number of books that

[3] The number, as of 1952, was 4,126. An interesting breakdown according to half centuries shows the number of books condemned in each period: 1600–49:469; 1650–99:862; 1700–49:723; 1750–99:463; 1800–49:576; 1850–99:778; 1900–49:255. These figures are taken from *What Is the Index*, by Redmond A. Burke, C.S.V. (Milwaukee: Bruce, 1952), p. 52.

have been given the dubious distinction of being placed on the Index is rather on the infinitesimal side compared to the number of titles issued through the centuries. This fact in itself is indicative of the restraint with which Rome works in the matter of restricting the freedom of members of the Church in the field of reading.

Further, of these four thousand books, probably two thirds are technical, professional works, many of which are unknown even to workers in the same professional fields and which probably could not be found outside an extremely antiquarian library. A surprising feature of the titles on the Index—surprising to those who are not familiar with the nature of the Index—is the fact that most of the proscribed works in theology and philosophy were written by priests. In the whole field of literature, in which Catholic readers might probably feel that their freedom was being most restricted, there are not more than several hundred titles on the Index. The national literature that leads the field is the French—Zola, Balzac, Hugo, to name a few, have some or all of their works on the Index. There is only one English novel on the list—Richardson's *Pamela* (Sterne's *Sentimental Journey* is named, too, if one would call it a novel)—and not a single American novel has been listed; in fact, there are but few American-authored books of any type in the roster.

The charge, then, so frequently heard, that the existence of the Index is a paralyzing restraint on the intellectual freedom of Catholics is surely a much-too-sweeping indictment. The average Catholic would be inclined or tempted to read but very few titles on the Index even if all its restrictions were lifted tomorrow. Further, as we shall see later, the restrictions of the Index are not absolute. If one objects *in principle* to the Index, then, of course, the restrictions it imposes are unjustifiable; but if one approves the general principles that some restrictions are possible and even necessary, and that the Church has the authority so to limit the freedom of its members for a greater good, then the wonder grows that the Index is so temperate in tone and minimum in extension. Certainly its scope lends no color to the suspicion of tyranny over intellectual freedom. Incidentally, the Index is not a deep, dark secret; it is an actual book which can be purchased in most

Catholic bookstores and consulted in public libraries. Don't expect, however, that it will make very exciting reading; you will hardly be impelled to rush out to try to get permission to read Michael Amatus' (1725) *De Piscium atque Avium Esus Consuetudine apud quosdam Christi Fidelium in Antepaschali Jejunio* ("On the Customs of Some Christians of Eating Fish and Birds in the Pre-Easter Fast") or Gideon Harvey's (1701) *The Art of Curing Diseases by Expectation*. I am far from suggesting that the books on the Index are all quaint museum pieces; many of them, to be sure, are of little importance today, but in their times they posed a real threat to the faith and/or morals of the Catholic public to whom they were addressed. Several centuries from now many may wonder why Alberto Moravia was ever considered important enough to be placed on the Index, but Rome had a good reason for warning all, and especially the Catholics of Italy, of the distressing effects his books were having, with their despairing commentary on modern life.

The second mode of controlling books and reading is contained in two sections of Canon Law. In Canon 1385 there is a question of *censura praevia* (prior censorship). This applies to authors; Catholics, whether clerics or lay, may not publish books that explicitly deal with matters of faith or morals without permission from ecclesiastical authority. This permission is commonly sought from the bishop of the diocese in which the author resides (it can also be petitioned from the bishop of the diocese in which the book is either printed or published). Such treatments of faith and morals include, for instance, the Holy Scriptures or notes and commentaries on them; books on theology, philosophy (especially ethics), ecclesiastical history, books of prayer and devotion, and, in general, books in which "there is something of particular relevance to religion and public morals."

The procedure is as follows. The author submits his manuscript for pre-publication inspection by the "censors" of the diocese. As we shall see later, these are competent and carefully selected specialists. If, after careful consideration, they find nothing in the book that is opposed to faith or morals, they issue (they must do so, indeed) a *nihil obstat*. This Latin phrase means merely "there is nothing against" publication.

Acting on this decision of the experts, the bishop of the diocese in almost routine fashion appends his *imprimatur*, which means "let it be published." This official approval, let it be understood, does *not* mean that the bishop has necessarily read the book (he has his officials for the purpose), nor does it necessarily signify that the bishop is according the book his hearty approval. Indeed, there may well be, let us say, some overtones in the book that indicate that the author is of the Democratic party persuasion; a bishop who happens to be a devout Republican cannot for that reason refuse to give the book his *imprimatur*, though he may heartily disagree with every bray of the donkey that echoes in its pages. The *imprimatur* is, we may say, a negative approval; it simply means that the freedom of the author to publish is stated after a decision that nothing in the book is contrary to traditional Catholic teaching on faith and morals.

In Canon 1399 the restriction is shifted from *pre* to *post*: restrictions on reading books that are already published (and these normally, as is clear, will be by non-Catholic authors, save in the category of literature, when such books are forbidden by the Code).

There are twelve categories of books mentioned in Canon 1399 (the last category deals with printed pictures of Our Lord, the Blessed Virgin, the angels and saints and "other servants of God," when and if such representations are contrary to the "mind of the Church"). The other eleven categories are: editions or translations of the Holy Scriptures made by non-Catholics; books which propound heresy or schism or in any way attempt to subvert the very foundations of religion; books which have for their principle or one of their notable purposes to attack religion or right morals; books by non-Catholics which professedly treat of religion, unless there is nothing in them that is contrary to the Catholic faith; books of Holy Scriptures and commentaries concerning them and books of revelations, miracles, prophecies, and new devotions published without proper ecclesiastic permission; books which attack or ridicule any Catholic dogmas; books which approve superstition, magic, spiritism, and other such practices; books which favor divorce, suicide, and so on; books which purposely treat of or teach lascivious or obscene matters; liturgical books that have been so changed as not to agree with approved editions; books containing apocryphal indulgences.

As is obvious, the books forbidden here which touch most on the freedom of the average Catholic reader are the books on religion by non-Catholics and those which are *ex professo* (as the Canon puts it) obscene. Catholics do not generally have to be warned, nor are they actually interested in, books that attack their faith. Further, it should be noted that the rule for the "strict interpretation" of Canon Law still holds. When it is stated, for instance, that books that *propound* heresy are forbidden, the word must be taken to mean "to promote or defend by argument"; it would be an unlawful extension of the meaning to widen it to include an incidental reference to heresy, even though the reference were favorable. Similar operative words in the Canon are to be interpreted in their minimum sense. It would carry us far afield in the present work to comment on all such words in the law; one who is interested in pursuing the matter further has but to consult any commentary on Canon Law or specifically any book on the portions of Canon Law that deal with this matter of the censorship and prohibition of books.[4] The meaning of the word "obscene" will occupy our attention at some length later.

Who has the power so to restrict the freedom of the Catholic to read? Not every official in the Church. The Holy See can, of course, declare books forbidden for the universal Church; this is commonly done by a decree of the Holy Office, one of the Roman congregations. A bishop may forbid a book to the reading of members of his diocese, wherein, for instance, a particular book is causing danger to souls because of peculiar circumstances. No parish priest or pastor, however, has this power; he may, and sometimes must, counsel against the reading of a particular book, but it is not within his power to forbid it unless it clearly falls within the provisions of Canon Law, or would probably be a serious temptation to a

[4] Such, for example, as Bouscaren and Ellis, *Canon Law: A Text and Commentary* (Milwaukee: Bruce, 1946), or Redmond A. Burke, *op. cit.*

particular individual. If we may recall the famous case of Betty Smith's *A Tree Grows in Brooklyn*, no Catholic priest had the power to *forbid* (in the sense of establishing a law) the reading of the book, however much he may have found it distasteful, vulgar, or "common"; it clearly did not fall in the category of an "obscene" book, as Canon Law understands that word; the priest might have dissuaded its reading, but beyond that he could not, in justice, have gone.

The obligation laid on Catholics to abide by the restrictions of Canon Law in the matter of reading is a serious obligation, for the simple reason that the purpose of the law is serious —namely, to safeguard Catholic dogma and Christian morals. To clarify this obligation, it is perhaps necessary to say a few words on the nature and binding-power of "positive" legislation. This is legislation which defines and specifies obligations that already exist through the natural moral law. This natural law—man's recognition of God's eternal law—demands, for example, good social relations if one is going to live in a society. The state will step in and say, "Well and good, but in order to be a good citizen, you will have to obey some traffic regulations," and accordingly makes some positive laws about speed and so on. Canon Law is likewise positive law; it defines and specifies the general law that Catholics should be good Catholics, holding fast to faith and living according to sound morals. To abide by the disciplinary regulations of Canon Law is a *means* to achieve the end.

Now, positive law, whether ecclesiastical or civil, binds *all* members of its own society—Church or state—precisely because it is legislation for the common good. It may be that a particular individual *knows* that the law is not necessary for him; a man may know that he is the world's safest driver and that therefore he can drive at eighty miles an hour with positively no danger to the life or limb of anyone. Well, he still *may* not drive that fast where the law says fifty miles is the limit; if he does, he breaks the law and is subject to fine, protest as he may that he is above the law. The reason, obviously, is that the law has to be based on the objective common good and not on one's subjective interpretation of what the law ought to be to fit his particular case. It is far better to restrict the freedom of an individual than to permit every individual to be a law unto himself, for that way lies social chaos.

The same character of positive law obtains when that positive law is ecclesiastical. It may be that an individual knows with sincere and complete conviction that if he reads a book that is a most blatant attack on the Catholic dogmas he holds with all his heart he would not for an instant find his faith being insidiously undermined. It could be—though self-deception is an easy state of mind to slide into. But, granted the truth of the supposition, it does not matter; the law still binds, for it was made for the common good and cannot take into consideration the peculiar gifts or strength of character of the individual. The only way anyone, whether in ecclesiastical or civil life, can get a relaxation from the positive law is to go to the lawmaker and get a statement that the particular law does not bind him. If you can flash a certificate signed by mayor, police department, traffic-control bureau, and whatever other agency is necessary, then you may drive at eighty miles; otherwise you will be smitten with a fine every time you are caught. So it is with the obligation of Catholics with respect to restrictions on reading, and this leads us to the point mentioned above; namely, that the limitation of reading, whether expressed in the Index or in the twelve categories of books, is not *absolute*.

This is a part of the picture that is rarely adverted to when our non-Catholic friends refer to the supposed intellectual shackles that fetter Catholic intellectual freedom. The statement always runs, "But there are *so many* books you Catholics *can't* read," whereas it ought to be something like, "There are, aren't there, some books you have to get permission to read?" For the possibility of obtaining permission is written right into the Code.[5] In ordinary cases, permission to read forbidden books is obtained through one's bishop, and permission will not be granted unless there is a good and sufficient reason for the book to be read. One engaged in professional literary work, for instance, might really find it necessary to read all the works of Zola, let us say. Again, if one were teaching the

[5] Cf., for example, Bouscaren and Ellis, *op. cit.*, pp. 724–25.

history of religions, it would probably be of prime importance to him to know many of the classic works that propound (i.e., "promote and defend by argument") heretical doctrines. But if there is good reason for the book to be read, and if (obviously a necessary condition, else the permission would defeat the very end and purpose of the law) the danger to the prospective reader's faith and morals is not discernible, permission is as a rule fairly easy to get. It must be added, however, that *no one*—not even the Pope of Rome—can give *anyone* permission to read a book whose reading would be a sin, would place the reader in proximate spiritual danger. If one has permission to read a book and still finds that he cannot "take" the book, his conscience obliges him to stop reading it, and he will sin if he violates the mandate of his conscience. Exemptions from the positive law do not ever carry with them license to violate the natural moral law. So our friend who has all the legal permissions in the world to drive eighty miles an hour has to stop it when he finds that his reflexes are slowing up and he is endangering his own and others' necks; otherwise, despite what his permission grants, he will be in his own conscience (if an accident happens) guilty of manslaughter and/or suicide.

Let us return for some consideration of the *censura praevia*. This is, as we have seen, the only real censorship in the strict sense of the word. In most of the discussion in this country on the problems of censorship, the question really hinges, not on prior censorship of books, but on the possibility and advisability of their control *after* publication. But since prior censorship is apparently so repellent to many, it may be worth while to examine the spirit in which the Church exercises it. If we keep in mind the points that have already been established about the presumption in favor of freedom, about the higher freedom that is always envisioned in any restrictions of freedom, and so on, it will not come as a surprise to anyone that the Church, while demanding prior examination of some books before permission is granted to publish, is reasonable in the provisions it sets up.

The rules for censors which are laid down in the Code, and which apply both to censors of the Roman Congregation of the Holy Office and to censors in the various dioceses as well, may be summarized as follows. Censors are to be well versed in the subject with which the book under examination treats, as well as with the language in which it is written. In the performance of their office they must "put aside all undue influence that might arise from a consideration of persons and attend only to the dogmas of the Church and to common Catholic doctrine. It is clear from this that censors are not to judge according to their private opinions or the tenets of a favorite school, but according to *common* Catholic doctrine . . ." If they judge that a book is sound in doctrine but that its publication may, for some reason or other, be inopportune, they may give their opinion as to the inopportuneness, but must, at the same time, clearly approve publication as regards soundness of doctrine. Wherever possible, leniency must be shown, and if a book is refused clearance under the phrase *donec corrigatur* (until corrections be made), the author must be heard in his own defense and the fact that the book was so refused clearance must not be publicized if the author agrees to correct the passages that violate the common teaching of the Church. Finally, any strictures that may have been leveled against the book are to be secret between the author and the examiners and not revealed even to the author's representatives, unless the author agrees. In this way, the legislation, while preserving the purity of Catholic teaching, endeavors with all its power to preserve the author's good name and to give him every possible benefit of the doubt. This is, to be sure, censorship in the strict sense, which the Church must, from its very nature, exercise; but it would be captious to deny that it is censorship exercised with prudence, consideration, and charity.

The history of the Roman Index of Forbidden Books is a fascinating field for exploration, manifesting the perennial concern of the Church to strike a balance between purity of doctrine on the one hand and freedom of inquiry on the other. It is a history, however, that is too long to be covered in these pages. We shall attempt, therefore, to give some highlights which may serve to show the spirit of the Church in its disciplinary legislation and the enforcement of that legislation.

There are allusions to types of "censorship" in the Christian dispensation as far back as apostolic times. In the Acts of the Apostles (19:19) and in St. Paul's Epistle to Titus (3:10), to cite but two instances, there are references to writings that Christians are urged not to read or forbidden to read. The first formal condemnation of a book, however, occurs in A.D. 325, when the first Council of Nicea anathematized the heresiarch Arius and his book *Thalia*. The *Decretum Gelasianum* (496), which is sometimes called "the first Roman Index," condemned scriptural apocrypha, books propounding heresies, forged acts of the Christian martyrs, spurious penitentials, and books propagating superstitions. In the thirteenth century we come across the first decrees from Rome and from diocesan councils forbidding unauthorized translations of the Bible and the reading of them. (In this connection it is worthy to note that a general prohibition against Catholics reading the Bible has never existed—contrary to popular modern opinion.) These were all instances of *censura repressiva*—prohibition to read books already published.

It was not until the rise of the religious turmoil that preceded the Reformation, and was rendered more widespread by the invention of printing, that *censura praevia* (prior censorship) came into effect. Again it is an interesting side light on history and particularly on much modern suspicion that Rome itself must be the source of all "repressions of human freedom" to note that the first instances of prior censorship occurred in Germany, where the religious unrest was most plaguing religious and secular authorities. Cologne gives us the first example in 1497, followed by Würzburg in 1482 and Mainz in 1485. Various papal documents deal with the problem of censorship (Innocent VIII in 1487, Leo X in 1515), but it was not until 1559 that Paul IV promulgated a list of forbidden books which was to apply universally and which was the first such list called an "Index." The key document in the whole history of the Index, however, and the one most indicative of the judicious atmosphere in which condemnation of books is weighed, is the bull *Sollicita ac Provida* of Benedict XIV (1753). This has been said to be the best source for "refutation of charges against the legislation"; for one thing, "it represented on the whole a relaxation of the strictness which had hitherto prevailed."[6] Finally, in 1908, Pius X, in reorganizing the Roman congregations, made no changes respecting the Congregation of the Index (which had been merged with the Congregation of the Holy Office) and confirmed the bull of Benedict XIV. It is this legislation of 1753, accordingly, under which the Church operates today in both types of censorship, *praevia* and *repressiva*.

These three chapters taken together will establish, we trust, *the* Catholic viewpoint on censorship. This view entails a concept of law and a concept of freedom under law. These two concepts are preserved and applied in the *official* legislation of the Church in the way and in the spirit we have tried to indicate. When one is asked, "What does *the Church* think of censorship?" one can only respond, "Let's look at the law and its spirit." Obviously, in the application of that law to a particular country and to a particular age, there will be variations—never in essentials, but in accidentals. But *the Church* speaking in its official capacity, has no opinion on the operations of civil censorship. Not on the *operations*; but the Church may very well have strong opinions on a philosophy that underlies either censorship or the lack of it. The whole tradition and spirit of the Church would deny that legitimate governments have no *right* to censor for the common good; that tradition and spirit would indeed assert the *duty* of such governments to censor for that same good. On the other hand, the Church would deny the *right* of any government to censor any truth—intellectual or moral—as a matter of policy, or to broadcast any error in the same manner.

[6] Ludwig Von Pastor, *The History of the Popes from the Close of the Middle Ages* (St. Louis: Herder, 1949), Vol. XXXV, p. 359. The whole section (pp. 346–63) is most instructive in its discussion of Benedict's liberal attitude. It is this Pope who laid down the prudent and charitable rules to govern censors which we have summarized on pp. 58–59.

CHAPTER IV

"Obscenity"—An Example of Interpretation

As an illustration of the "strict interpretation" that is enjoined
by Canon Law, it may be well to develop the evolution of
the meaning of the word "obscene" or "obscenity" as it is
understood in the Catholic view on censorship. This will not
only be a historical note but will be seen to have an immediate
bearing on our current debate on censorship. This is true because most of the material on our newsstands (and on the
screen as well) which comes under attack by those who favor
some forms of social control does so precisely because it is
called "immoral," "suggestive," "indecent," or something else
of that nature. These labels arouse in the mind of the ordinary
observer the suspicion that such material is being called "obscene." "Obscenity" in a very wide sense, therefore, may be
said to be the nub of the controversy. The anti-censorship
faction must not be thought to be immoralists who look with a
kindly eye on the dissemination of "obscenity"; the vast majority in this camp are, we must suppose, good, decent citizens
who abhor obscenity. Their quarrel with the pro-censorship
camp lies in their sincere conviction that even language and
depictions that are (or very close to) obscene must be allowed,
under our constitutional guarantee of freedom of speech and
the press, to circulate freely until such time as they can be
effectively curtailed in a local situation by full and due process
of legal trial and conviction. The pro-censorship people, on
the other hand, think that by the time such legal procedures
have been gone through with, incalculable harm to society,
and especially to the young, will already have been done; they
seek a method to minimize the harm while indeed waiting
for and hoping for full relief through full legal procedures.
We may perhaps sum it up by saying that the pro-censorship
group thinks that the *antis* are willing to settle for too little
too late; the anti-censorship group is convinced that the *pros*
are asking for too much too soon.

Further, this chapter will have especial relevance in view of the United States Supreme Court decision of June 24, 1957, which held, in three cases decided by split decisions, that the freedom of speech and the press constitutionally protected under the First and Fourteenth Amendments does not include "obscenity."

Periculosum est definire, runs the cautionary Latin tag. "It's dangerous to make definitions," because, philosophically speaking, a definition should fit *omni et soli*; that is, *every* case that falls within the scope of the class to be defined and *only* those cases. A horse is not defined by being called an animal; he must be differentiated from every other animal by such qualifications that the definition fits only horses and all horses. Despite this difficulty—which, obviously, is thornier in a matter of moral action than in the field of physical characteristics—canonists and moral theologians have attempted a strict definition of "obscenity." Their efforts are worth dwelling on, because they illustrate admirably the caution and prudence with which Canon Law goes about determining restrictions on human liberty. This attitude of saving freedom as far as possible in particular circumstances must be operative in the activities of groups who engage in concrete attempts at censorship; it ought also to engender respect in those who are inclined to think, often without any precise information on the subject, that the Catholic Church is all too ready to "throw its weight around." As we shall see, the Church does not engage in such gymnastic activity even in regard to its own members; much less does it seek to control and restrict the freedom of those who are not among its convinced followers.

What, then, is "obscenity" in the teaching of Canon lawyers and moral theologians? First of all, Canon Law itself does not define the obscene. In its legislation that restricts to some degree and in some circumstances the freedom of Catholics to read, one class of books forbidden is those that are *ex professo* obscene. But the law itself does not say what the "obscene" is. To discover this we have to go to authoritative interpretations. It ought not come as a surprise that obscenity is not defined in the Code. The ecclesiastical legal minds who gave us the Code of Canon Law were at pains to forestall, as lawyers must always be, any ambiguities and possible sources of misunderstanding. When, therefore, they did not spell out the meaning of the word "obscene," it can legitimately be supposed that the canonists did not conceive that the word was complicated or obscure. They took it for granted, as it were, that the word was rather self-evident. It would seem that only in a pluralistic society such as ours today has the problem arisen as to the precise meaning of obscenity. But the problem has arisen, and commentators on the Code have grappled with it.

We may approach their attempts at precise definition by delimiting the field negatively. Our starting point can well be the remark by a famous moral theologian, Reverend Arthur Vermeersch, S.J. Referring to the visual arts (but with obvious application to literature), he states: "Not every nude can be called obscene; in common estimate, an obscene nude is a nude that allures, and obscenity may be defined as a 'degrading manifestation of the mind (of the author—painter, sculptor, writer) or a degrading solicitation of the mind (of the viewer or reader) in and through the nudity.' "[1] We may not have got very far, but at least we have taken a step in the right direction. The question now arises: In precisely what does the "degrading" element consist?

It consists in the intrinsic tendency or bent of the work to arouse sexual passion, or, to put it more concretely, the motions of the genital apparatus which are preparatory to the complete act of sexual union. It must be noted that a particular work—the book, the statue, and so on—may not always and in all circumstances so arouse this or that individual. The same person may now actually be aroused, or on another occasion (when he is unwell, let us say, or physically sluggish) not actually be aroused. It is not so much a matter of the individual's own reaction here and now as the nature of the work under consideration. And it must be the *intrinsic* nature of the work, not an accidental circumstance. So, for example, one of perverse moral character or abnormal sexual excitability

[1] Arthur Vermeersch, *Theologia Moralis* (Rome, 1926), p. 94. The phrase runs in the original: *"Non omne nudum dici potest obscenum; sed vulgo dicitur obscenum nudum allectans et dici potest: turpis in nuditate manifestatio animi vel sollicitatio."*

might possibly be sexually aroused by stroking a rose petal or a piece of velvet, but no one would call either object obscene.

Further, the sexual arousement need not actually follow the contemplation of the object that is obscene. In Catholic sex morality, the deliberate arousal of sexual thoughts that are of their nature destined to be preparatory to sexual stimulation and the complete act is of itself a serious sin. Perhaps this needs some further explanation. The simple principle is this: "The importance of the *degree* of the sex activity that has been aroused does not enter into the reckoning of the gravity of the sin." To clarify this by an example:

"Thus, pressing the button of a small electric switch can start the most powerful machinery. The least voluntary degree of sex activity is like a switch that brings into action beyond our power of control 'primordial forces that move in the depths of our nature.' If it is always gravely sinful to bring these forces into action, except in conformity to moral law [that is to say, in their proper activity in wedlock], it must be equally sinful to do what is to them the same as pressing the starting-switch is to all the machinery connected with it. It does not matter whether this activity be physical or mental ('bad thoughts'), for both kinds have the same effect on the deeper forces connected with them; that is, of course, provided they are voluntary."[2]

This is called by the theologians "venereal pleasure," and in summary we may say that if a work is to be called obscene it must, of its nature, be such as actually to arouse or calculated to arouse in the viewer or reader such venereal pleasure. If the work is *not* of such a kind, it may, indeed, be vulgar, disgusting, crude, unpleasant, what you will—but it will *not* be, in the strict sense which Canon Law obliges us to apply, obscene. Let us repeat, this interpretation is by no means an apology or excuse for vulgar and disgusting works, and Catholic groups are well within their moral and legal rights when they protest the presence of such stuff for general consumption. But it is a reminder that, since a restriction of human

[2] E. Mersch, *Love, Marriage and Chastity* (New York: Sheed and Ward, 1939), p. 19. These notes in the book are by the translator, one A.S.

liberty is here at stake, that liberty must be and can be restricted only as far as is necessary for the attainment of a higher good. Indulgence in vulgarity may or may not be a sin, depending on circumstances; indulgence in obscenity is always a sin, and freedom from temptation to that sin is the higher good the law envisions and protects.

There is a further question that arises. It is possible, is it not, that obscenity (in the limited sense in which we have defined it) may be present in a book or a film in an accidental or transient fashion? How do we judge whether the book *as a whole* is to be considered obscene? Here again Canon Law indulges in no wide, all-comprehensive, blanket condemnations. The words of the law say a book is forbidden reading for Catholics if it is *ex professo* obscene. What does this mean? Father H. Noldin, S.J., an eminent moral theologian, has explained: "For a book to be prohibited [by reason of its obscenity], it is necessary that from its whole tenor the author's intention is evident of teaching the reader about sins of impurity and arousing him to libidinousness."[3] Further comments on the "whole nature" of the work, found in many works, include the fact that "useful books imparting scientific information do not deal *designedly* with obscene matter as such and so do not fall within this category" of forbidden books.[4] Finally, to provide a prudential rule of action, the question "How much?" must be answered. How often can the author slip in his "accidental" obscenities before one is forced to the conclusion that they are not accidental at all, but designed to give a certain tone and flavor to the whole work? The commentators we have been quoting say cautiously that the author's intention to arouse libidinous thoughts and consequent actions may be presumed if a "considerable" part of the work clearly manifests such a slant. What is "considerable"? "It is the general contention that a book containing

[3] *De Preceptis Dei et Ecclesiae* (Innsbruck, 1926), p. 658. The Latin text: "*Ut prohibitus sit liber, requiritur ut ex tota ejus indole appareat scribentis intentionem lectorem de peccatis turpibus instruendi et ad libidinem excitandi.*"

[4] Cf., for example, John A. Abbo and Jerome D. Hannan, *The Sacred Canons* (St. Louis: Herder, 1952), p. 638.

one full chapter which is obscene falls under this general prohibition."[5]

In these various ways does Canon Law, which contains, as we have said, *the* Catholic viewpoint on censorship, proceed temperately and wisely. It will not broaden the definition of "the obscene" so as to include anything and everything to which a decent-minded and sensitive person may object; it will not condemn a book because of an isolated passage; it makes no equation, for instance, between a portrayal of sin in literature and "teaching about sins of impurity." Certainly, Catholics, whether in their individual thinking or in any group action, have to be guided by this spirit and letter of Canon Law. An individual Catholic may and should determine to avoid any reading at all that is indelicate, of low taste, not fit for gentle men and women (what a "quaint" phrase, but how lovely!) and, in the words of St. Paul, we can only say, "*In hoc laudo* [For this I praise you]." But no Catholic can *impose* on himself or others, or counsel others that they must follow, *as a disciplinary law of the Catholic Church*, any law stricter than the one laid down by supreme spiritual authority and interpreted by authoritative commentators.

[5] Burke, *op. cit.*, p. 37. Father Burke remarks, and we add his statement here for the guidance of those who may want to know what to do in a particular circumstance, that "it may happen that an individual in reading comes across an obscene passage. This he may skip and continue reading." Obviously, however, if such passages keep recurring to such a degree that they set up a temptation for the individual reader, his conscience may oblige him to put the book aside completely, though it may not be, technically, an obscene book. Recall what was said in Chapter III about the obligations of the positive and natural law.

PART II

THE CENSORSHIP CONTROVERSY IN THE UNITED STATES

CHAPTER I

The Legal Climate

It may safely be stated that the prevailing climate in the courts in this country is rather hostile to overt attempts at censorship, particularly of the printed word. Time after time, local courts and even the Supreme Court of the United States have intervened to protect freedom of speech that seemed to be endangered by hasty or ill-defined action on the part of local police officials, district attorneys, and so on. This is not the place, nor is there space enough, to attempt a detailed résumé of such vindications of freedom of speech under our constitutional guarantees. The reader may be referred, if he cares to keep abreast of such court protection, to the *Censorship Bulletins* of the American Book Publishers Council, which month by month keeps a vigilant eye on any attempts at censorship, whether by the National Office for Decent Literature or by any other group or law-enforcement agencies.

Two observations, however, are germane to this brief survey of the legal climate. First, though many individual cases have been adjudicated in favor of freedom of speech, the *general* principle of censorship has not been called into question by the courts. It is difficult to see how it could be called into question, for almost every civilized modern country has on its books laws destined to forbid or strictly curtail the dissemination of obscene literature, mainly, it is true, in the field of using the mails for distribution. There is an international agreement among some fifty nations, called an "Agreement for the Suppression of the Circulation of Obscene Publications," to which the United States is a signatory. All fifty states of the Union have "obscenity laws,"[1] and since 1942 no less

---

[1] New Mexico has no general obscenity statute, but it does have a statute giving to municipalities the power "to prohibit the sale or exhibiting of obscene or immoral publications, prints, pictures or illustrations."

than twenty obscenity laws have been enacted by the Congress of the United States. In other words, there would seem to be a universal and natural revulsion against obscenity, in the printed word as well as in act, a general recognition of its deleterious effect on society, and a determination to extirpate or at least control it. Censorship, consequently, at least to this extent, seems implicit in the very constitution of any modern state.[2] It is hard to see how the out-and-out opponents of the very principle of censorship can square the realities of modern social life with the ideal of some utopian freedom of speech.

Modern states, however, have continually run into legal difficulties in establishing and maintaining a definition of obscenity that does the twofold job of forestalling a social and moral evil and not unduly interfering with social liberty. This is no place to examine these continual difficulties as they have arisen in all lands. It will be helpful, however, to dwell a bit on the solution of the twofold problem as it has arisen and been handled in England and our own country, for such a consideration will bring us to the second of our two general observations. It is this: many American Catholics have expressed the fear that our courts, and even the Supreme Court, have been "letting down the bars" too much in their attitudes toward controlling indecency in literature and the films. The laxity may be a fact, but a Catholic attitude toward censorship must, as we have been saying in the first part of this book, be shaped according to the spirit of Canon Law. Now, as the preceding chapter has shown, Canon Law endeavors to be most precise in its use of words: "vulgarity," for instance, is not "obscenity." Most of our court decisions have hinged exactly on this point; namely, that the charges against a book or a film have been too imprecise and vague to assure "due process." It is all very well to think that "anybody knows" what "indecency" is, but when it comes to the crux of depriving

[2] The most thorough treatment, to my knowledge, of the entire question of this aspect of "freedom of speech" in modern society is *Obscenity and the Law*, by Norman St. John-Stevas (New York: Macmillan, 1956). The book is a fascinating survey of history, social customs, the law, and all other aspects of the problem. It is particularly valuable for its appendices, especially the one on comparative law, in which one may find the obscenity statutes in all modern countries.

someone of freedom of action, of curtailing his civic liberty by process of law, it is imperative that the word be susceptible of a quite precise meaning. As Catholics, we ought to be very conscious of the importance of clear definitions: we have had enough experience by now in the vagaries of the "separation" of Church and state to realize that for legal purposes the precision of Canon Law is a great desideratum on the American legal scene. Further, since our American society is pluralistic —religious and moral truths, standards, values are not universally agreed upon—it is of the utmost importance that the law, in acting on a definition that will please one minority group, does not impose a penalty on other groups. We ought, accordingly, not become too alarmed when we read in the press headlines, as we do from time to time, that "censorship has been struck another mortal blow" by such-and-such a decision. It is precisely because the courts are so slow and, as some would charge, lax in this matter that the social dynamism of such organizations as the Legion of Decency and the National Office for Decent Literature is so necessary.

Be that as it may, a recent development in legal thinking in this country has somewhat changed the prevailing legal climate respecting censorship. It is a heartening change, for it indicates that, whatever the difficulties of definition in the field of censorship in a pluralistic society, some words at least are precise enough in general estimation to assure due process of law. In other words, this recent legal development has implicitly stated that though the definition of some words in a pluralistic society is hard to come by, there is still enough moral consensus even in such a society to vindicate the moral content of such a word, for instance, as "obscenity." In still other words, the natural moral law is at times a sufficient basis for just, temperate, and necessary censorship.

Let us examine briefly this evolution of the legal meaning of the word "obscenity." Not only will our inspection illuminate this recent change in United States legal thinking; it will manifest the striking parallelism between Canon and civil law.

In England the working definition of obscenity that was universally applied in modern times had been the work of Lord Chief Justice Cockburn. In a famous case (*Regina* v. *Hicklin*, 1868) Mr. Justice Cockburn had laid down this test of obscenity: "Whether the tendency of the matter charged as obscene is to deprave and corrupt those whose minds are open to such immoral influence, and into whose hands a publication of this sort may fall."[3]

In 1954, however, this test was challenged, in the case of *Regina* v. *Martin Secker and Warburg, Ltd.*, as tending, in the words of the United States Supreme Court decision of June 24, 1957, "to allow material to be judged [obscene] merely by the effect of an isolated passage upon particularly susceptible persons."[4] These "legally infirm" elements in the Hicklin test have been rejected by many state decisions here. In the famous *Ulysses* case, for example, in 1933, the U. S. Court of Appeals upheld the ruling of Judge John M. Woolsey that the book was not pornographic and in so doing broadened the base for a definition of obscenity when it said: "The same immunity should apply to literature as to science, where the presentation, viewed objectively, is sincere, and the erotic matter is not introduced to promote lust and does not furnish the dominant note of the publication. The question in each case is whether the publication *taken as a whole* [emphasis added] has a libidinous effect."[5]

Here we have the first obvious parallel between the civil and Canon law. Judge Woolsey's "taken as a whole" is Father Noldin's "whole tenor" of the book; the judge's "dominant note" is the same norm as the universal criterion of the moralists, *ex tota ejus indole, ex tota natura*, both of which parallels have been treated above.

But a further significant step was taken by our Supreme Court in its 1957 ruling. In addition to stating that the work charged as obscene must be judged as a whole and not from isolated passages, the bench considered the matter of the readers of such a work. Mr. Justice William J. Brennan, Jr., who

[3] St. John-Stevas, *op. cit.*, pp. 69–70 and notes, gives a full account of this celebrated case.

[4] *Roth* v. *United States*, 354 U.S. 476 (1957). This is the source of all subsequent references to the June 24 decision.

[5] *U.S.* v. *One Book Called Ulysses*. Judge Woolsey's famous decision may most conveniently be consulted in the Modern Library edition of James Joyce's *Ulysses* (1942), where it is printed in full with an introduction by Morris L. Ernst.

handed down the decision in the *Roth* v. *United States* case,[6] quoted with approval the approach to the definition of obscenity that had been employed by the trial courts which had condemned both litigants:

". . . In the Alberts case, in ruling on a motion to dismiss, the trial judge indicated that, as the trier of facts, he was judging each item as a whole as it would affect the normal person, and in *Roth*, the trial judge instructed the jury as follows: '. . . The test is not whether it (the material charged as obscene) would arouse sexual desires or sexual impure thoughts in those comprising a particular segment of the community, the young, the immature or the highly prudish or would leave another segment, the scientific or highly educated or the so-called worldly-wise and sophisticated indifferent and unmoved . . .

" 'The test in each case is the effect of the book, picture or publication considered as a whole, not upon any particular class, but upon all those whom it is likely to reach. In other words, you determine its impact upon the average person in the community. The books, pictures and circulars must be judged as a whole, in their entire context, and you are not to

[6] Three cases were handled in this decision: the Roth and Alberts cases and the case of Kingsley Books, Inc. We shall refer to the third case later in this chapter. In the first, Samuel Roth, a New York bookseller, had been convicted by jury trial in a New York district court of mailing obscene matter in violation of federal law. The conviction, which carries the penalty of fine and/or imprisonment, was upheld by the Court of Appeals for the Second Circuit. It was carried to the Supreme Court on the ground that the federal statute against using the mails to forward obscene matter is itself a violation of the First Amendment, which states that "Congress shall make no law . . . abridging the freedom of speech or of the press." The second case concerned one David S. Alberts, who conducted a mail-order business in Los Angeles. He had been convicted by a municipal court judge (having waived a jury trial) of "lewdly keeping for sale obscene and indecent books, and with writing and composing and publishing an obscene advertisement for them in violation of the California Penal Code." This conviction was sustained on appeal but reached the Supreme Court on the ground that Congress had pre-empted the regulatory field by enacting the federal statute against mailing obscene matter. The state, argued Alberts, had therefore no power to punish the "keeping for sale" or "advertising" of such materials. This argument was rejected by the Supreme Court.

consider detached or separate portions in reaching a conclusion. You judge [them] by present-day standards in the community. You may ask yourselves [if they] offend the common conscience of the community by present-day standards.

"'In this case, ladies and gentlemen of the jury, you and you alone are the exclusive judges of what the common conscience of the community is, and in determining that conscience you are to consider the community as a whole, young and old, educated and uneducated, the religious and the irreligious—men, women and children.'"[7]

Making these preceding tests of obscenity its own, the Supreme Court, in the words of Justice Brennan's decision, canonizes this definition of obscenity: "whether to the average person, applying contemporary community standards, the dominant theme of the material taken as a whole appeals to prurient interest." Here again we have those echoes from Canon Law. The "average person" in the estimate of the Court is the "person of normal sex instincts" to whom the moralists refer (they are fond of such expressions as *homo quadratus*; we would translate "the well-rounded man"). "Prurient interest" is clearly correlative to the "seductiveness" or "solicitation" in the work to which Father Vermeersch alludes.

The general conclusion reached by these three Supreme Court decisions is that the freedoms of speech and of the press guaranteed by the First and Fourteenth Amendments do not extend to obscene speech, taken in the sense in which the Court has defined it immediately above. The importance of the decisions lies in the fact that this is the first time that this issue has been squarely presented to our highest tribunal. The decision by the Supreme Court will naturally filter down into future decisions by local courts, and the whole approach to the question of censorship will, it is to be thought, take on a different complexion. This is not the place to go into all the argumentation of the Court, and especially into all the ramifications of the dissenting opinions. Whatever the weight of those opinions, the law of the land, following the Court's stand on June 24, 1957, is simply that obscenity does not fall within the boundaries of "free speech" as constitutionally understood;

[7] 354 U.S. 476 (1957).

that obscene speech is therefore illegal and punishable either after a judge's decision or jury trial; and that obscene speech (in written form: that is all the decisions were concerned with) may even, under certain circumstances, be legally subject to "prior" censorship.

This aspect of prior censorship was touched on in Mr. Justice Frankfurter's ruling in the Kingsley Books, Inc. case. It is of special significance because prior censorship is the particular horror of those who oppose censorship in general. In the case, copies of a book alleged to be obscene had been seized in New York and a court injunction had impeded further sale. Following court examination, the book was declared obscene and the firm was convicted under the state obscenity laws. Appeal was made to the Supreme Court on the ground that the restraining injunction was "prior censorship." Mr. Frankfurter, however, stated, and in doing so reminded all that prior censorship, even of the printed word, is not always and in all circumstances unconstitutional:

"Just as *Near* v. *Minnesota*, one of the landmark opinions in shaping the constitutional protection of freedom of speech and of the press, left no doubts that 'liberty of speech, and of the press, is also not an absolute right' . . . it likewise made clear that 'the protection even as to previous restraint is not absolutely unlimited.' "[8]

It may be of interest and pertinent to our specific discussion to outline briefly the grounds on which the Court reached its decision. This is so because the emphasis of the decisions was based on what may well be called the common-sense aspects of legal tradition. The Court's decision first of all gave some historical background in the shape of laws against obscenity going as far back as 1712 in Massachusetts. The decision's text then goes on:

"In the light of this history, it is apparent that the unconditional phrasing of the First Amendment ('Congress shall make no law . . . abridging the freedom of speech, or of the press') was not intended to protect every utterance. . . .

"The protection given speech and press was fashioned to assure unfettered interchange of ideas for the bringing about

8 *Op. cit.*

of political and social changes desired by the people. . . .

"All ideas having even the slightest redeeming social importance—unorthodox ideas, controversial ideas, even ideas hateful to the prevailing climate of opinion—have the full protection of the guaranties. . . . But implicit in the history of the First Amendment is the rejection of obscenity as utterly without redeeming social importance."

The decision then goes on to quote in support of this view a prior decision of the Supreme Court (*Chaplinsky* v. *New Hampshire*, 315 U.S. 568, 571–572):

". . . There are certain well-defined and narrowly limited classes of speech, the prevention and punishment of which has never been thought to raise any Constitutional problem. *These include the lewd and obscene . . . It has been well observed that such utterances are no essential part of any exposition of ideas, and are of such slight social value as a step to truth that any benefit that may be derived from them is clearly outweighed by the social interest in order and morality. . . .*" (The added emphasis is that of the present Court.)

An argument that was adduced to prove the unconstitutionality of obscenity laws, whether federal or state, was that such laws violate the guarantees because they make punishable *thoughts*, or rather material that is judged to be of such a nature that it incites to sexually impure *thoughts*, whether or not any overt act follows. There must be, this argument runs, at least a "clear and present danger" that overt acts will follow before the inciting obscenity can legally be declared punishable. The Court rejects that argument, on the ground that since obscene speech simply does not fall within the ambit of constitutional protection, the "clear and present danger" test is irrelevant. To support this contention, the Court again has recourse to legal precedent, quoting from *Beauharnais* v. *Illinois* (343 U.S. 250, 266):

"Libelous utterances not being within the area of constitutionally protected speech, it is unnecessary, either for us or for the State courts, to consider the issues behind the phrase 'clear and present danger.' *Certainly no one would contend that obscene speech, for example, may be punished only upon a showing of such circumstances.* Libel, as we have seen, is in the same class." (Emphasis added.)

All these elements being considered, the Court rejects another contention; namely, that the "obscenity" statues are so vague and imprecise that they do not "provide reasonably ascertainable standards of guilt and therefore violate the constitutional requirements of due process. . . . The thrust of the argument is that these words (obscene, lewd, lascivious, indecent and the like) are not sufficiently precise because they do not mean the same thing to all people, all the time, everywhere." To this argument the Court gives the following response, though restricting its application in the cases under review to the word "obscene":

"Many decisions have recognized that these decisions of obscenity statutes are not precise. This Court, however, has consistently held that lack of precision is not itself offensive to the requirements of due process. '. . . The Constitution does not require impossible standards'; all that is required is that the language 'conveys sufficiently definite warning as to the proscribed conduct when measured by common understanding and practices . . .' These words, applied according to the proper standard for judging obscenity, already discussed, give adequate warning of the conduct proscribed and mark . . . boundaries sufficiently distinct for judges and juries fairly to administer the law . . . That there may be marginal cases in which it is difficult to determine the side of the line on which a particular fact situation falls is no sufficient reason to hold the language too ambiguous to define a criminal offense . . .'"

Do we not seem to hear echoes of the eminently sensible and calm voice of St. Thomas Aquinas? "Human laws cannot have the unerring quality of scientifically demonstrated conclusions. Not every rule need possess final infallibility and certainty; as much as is possible in its class is enough" (*Summa Theologica*, 1a–2ae, xci. 3 ad 3); or again: "The statutes passed by a democracy may be just, not because they reach pure and complete justice, but because they fit the purpose of the regime" (Commentary, V *Ethics*, lect. 2); finally, "We must not seek the same degree of certainty in all things. Consequently, in contingent matters, such as natural and human things [human laws, and obscenity laws included] it is enough for a thing to be certain, as being true in the greater number of instances, though at times and less frequently it may fail."

This brief survey has been necessary so as to set the operations of the Legion of Decency and the NODL against the legal background in this country. If our courts, including the Supreme Court, seem to some to be slow and wavering in decisions against suggestiveness in the films and in literature, it must be said that at least they are not in favor of license. But their wheels do indeed grind slowly and many, especially Catholics, feel that the moral and social well-being of the country must have at its disposal readier means to combat the evil. Can those readier means be employed in keeping with the spirit of our Constitution, or are they almost of necessity doomed to transgress the spirit if not the letter of the law?

That is the problem to which we shall now turn. It may well be that many Catholics support the Legion and the NODL out of a feeling of impatience with our civil law. If so, perhaps they are expecting too much from legality, which can, at best, give but a minimum reinforcement to morality. Efforts to have laws against indecent and degrading films and books strengthened can certainly be made legitimately and laudably. One of the means to put teeth into such laws is at hand in the arousing of public opinion through the work of the Legion and the NODL. Is public opinion aroused by these two organizations a truly American public opinion? Let us see.

CHAPTER II

The National Legion of Decency

Our consideration thus far has been restricted to the principles that underlie a theory of censorship, an examination of the actual operation of a temperate and effective censorship as it is envisioned in the processes of Canon Law, and a brief survey of the legal climate in the United States as it currently surrounds the problems of censorship.

As a general conclusion of Part I, we arrived at the position that the official stand of the Church in matters of censorship and especially the spirit that animates that stand must be the guiding norm for any particular operations of censorship that may be embarked upon by Catholics, whether working as individuals or in groups which represent, to some degree or other, the attitude of the Church in a given era or locality. A Catholic group may be entirely unofficial, bearing no stamp at all of any ecclesiastical approbation or mandate; in this case, indeed, the use of the adjective "Catholic" is generally frowned on, as suggesting a degree of officialness which does not exist. Another Catholic group or organization may have a commission from, let us say, the bishop or bishops of a diocese or country. But whatever the group and whatever the degree of its official character, the spirit of the Church's formal legislation on the matter of censorship must animate and guide all the practical steps undertaken. Otherwise, any rash, injudicious, or intemperate measures employed will not only *not* mirror the mind of the Church but may actually and lamentably lead many to think that they are hearing the voice of the Catholic Church when all they hear is the perhaps ill-considered opinion of some self-constituted censors.

This is a field in which frankness and deference must work hand in hand. In delineating the work of two Catholic organizations that are engaged in trying to control indelicate (to say the very least) subject matter in the films and in printed material, there obviously must not be any founded suspicion that I am trying to tell those charged with the tasks how to manage their own organizations. Dangers of overzealousness, however, possible points of friction, perhaps needless, must be indicated if this book is to give a true picture of its subject matter.

The problem, then, may perhaps be stated thus: Do the Catholic organizations we shall consider in the rest of this book (1) live up to the spirit of Canon Law in their day-to-day operations? If they do, they certainly represent a valid Catholic viewpoint on censorship, though, by the very fact of their local limitations and applications, they cannot be called *the* Catholic viewpoint. (2) Granted such consonance with Canon Law, do these Catholic organizations work within the framework of the fundamental freedoms guaranteed by our Constitution, which Catholics, no less than any others, prize and cherish?

The two organizations to be examined are chosen because

they are most under attack as being "pressure groups" engaged in undemocratic and un-American suppression of the rights of free speech. They are the National Legion of Decency and the National Office for Decent Literature (to be referred to as the NODL). Are their purposes alien to freedom in a pluralistic society? Do their methods reflect the temper of the Church's official viewpoint on censorship? Is the criticism directed against them itself temperate and justified? Finally, is there any hope or chance that these two Catholic organizations can join forces with the vigorously anti-censorship elements in the country with a view to co-operation in drafting legislation, exercising persuasion on publishers and distributors, educating the public, and so on? There is untold good will on both sides—the American Civil Liberties Union, for instance, is not composed of lovers of pornography, and officials and members of the NODL are not dedicated to undermining American freedom. Both sides, it is to be assumed, recognize the problem and sense the good will, but neither side seems able to come up with any practical suggestions as to how to pool the good will. I am by no means sure that this book will reveal such suggestions, but if it does no more than give food for thought for both parties to the dispute, it may have served its purpose.

It must be remarked at the very outset that neither the Legion of Decency nor the NODL considers its own activities to be a species of censorship. Both organizations reply to charges that they are censoring by stating that their function is that of guiding the formation of public opinion, and that whatever repression or suppression of material (films or books) follows as a result of the formed opinion is secondary and, to a degree, accidental to their main purpose. There is a great deal of justification for such a position, for the function of both organizations *is* critical rather than suppressive. Now there is a sense in which a critic is inevitably a censor. When an Orville Prescott, for instance, reviews a book unfavorably in the New York *Times* and advises his readers not to waste their time or money on it, he is undoubtedly restricting the sale of the book. In this way he can be said to be "interfering" with the "freedom" of the author to have his book read by everyone. If a reviewer in a Catholic paper or journal were to review the same book and castigate it on moral grounds, presumably the Catholic followers of the reviewer would be even readier to stay away from the book in droves—and legitimate criticism would take on a form of "censorship." This censorial by-product of legitimate criticism is even more at work in the writing of drama critics. Many a play has been killed by a handful of caustic first-night notices.

This is to carry the implications of the word "censorship" to ridiculous extremes. Not even the opponents of censorship would extend it to a suppression of all criticism; yet it would seem that the principles on which they base their case against censorship ought logically to lead to such extremes. They escape the exaggerated conclusion by pointing out, with some justification, that a review like Mr. Prescott's does not, after all, *impose* his adverse judgment; one who seeks guidance from Mr. Prescott in his selection of reading matter may or may not follow the advice; he is still free to choose his reading matter. The more the criticism gets organized, the more the elements of censorship tend to emerge. Hence, when not just one critic but a board or a group issues the criticism, a form of social pressure is set up. This is acceptable if the pressure can be confined only to those members of society for whom the board or group is empowered to speak, but inevitably (so runs the argument) the social pressure tends to spill over beyond the engaged and committed members and to affect American society at large. Such organized criticism—which has now almost imperceptibly begun to be called censorship—tends to *impose* its judgment and will (a minority attitude) on those who may not agree either on the norms for the criticism or the necessity and advisability for the implementation of the criticism.

This is the problem that such Catholic organizations as the Legion and the NODL face. They must be free, as all admit, to persuade and even effectively urge Catholics to avoid the salacious, the indelicate, the vulgar (not to mention the obscene, which is already forbidden by the natural moral law) book or movie. But they are not free to *impose* their standards of judgment on those who are not subject to the discipline of the Church. But are they free to try to *persuade* those not subject to the Church's laws to agree with the standards and take part in positive action against such objectionable material? Again, the anti-censorship faction would probably say yes. The nub of their contention, however, is precisely here: they hold that what the Legion and the NODL contend to be persuasion is actually a disguised form of coercion. They seem to go even further by implying, if they do not come right out and say so, that these two Catholic organizations do not slip unintentionally, as it were, into coercion from time to time, but that coercion is what they really always have had in mind.

Now it is of no practical use whatever for Catholics in general simply to minimize such an implicit charge, nor is it the intention of this book to side-step the issues raised. For great principles are at stake, and if they will not be clarified in these pages, we may hope that at least a temperate and fruitful discussion will be advanced.

The first principle at stake is adverted to by St. Thomas in the statement we have adduced in the discussion of the role of coercion in law. There we stressed the educative, pedagogical aspect of coercion as one justification of the right and duty of censorship in either civil or ecclesiastical society. But if it is true that "there is a transition from coercion to persuasion,"[1] it is also true that there can easily arise a converse "transition from persuasion to coercion, and persuasion, as soon as it takes hold of the masses, gives birth to coercion. For instance, a campaign to influence public opinion, if successful, can eventually marshal coercive forces (strike, boycott, etc.)."[2]

The Legion and the NODL do not, they themselves claim (as we shall set forth in detail below), advocate coercion as regards the general American public. Some coercion is implied vis-à-vis Catholics, in so far as the specific actions of the two organizations remind Catholics of obligations they have, springing from the natural moral law. But on the general American scene both organizations deny that they are censorship bodies; they are agencies of organized criticism which

---

[1] Simon, *op. cit.*, p. 54, note 3, commenting on St. Thomas' teaching on the educative value of coercion.
[2] *Ibid.*

tries to arouse public opinion by methods of persuasion. But can it be that in their tactics of persuasion they have come (or may unconsciously come) to advocate or at least tolerate methods of coercion? Again, even if coercion were the aim and purpose of the Legion and the NODL, would it *ipso facto* constitute an un-American and undemocratic operation? If coercion were not that lamentable, could it still be a judicious and prudential way of achieving the goals of the organizations? These are some of the pressing questions.

The complete history of the Legion of Decency has yet to be published,[3] and when and if the entire record is put before the public, the account might well be a most fascinating and instructive sociological document. It would mirror, among many other social phenomena, changes in popular taste, the fluctuations within the movie industry between devotion to art and concern for the box office, the success or failure of specific films as a result of aroused indignant or commendatory public opinion, and so on. This is not the place for such a history, as we are concerned only with the relationship between the Legion and the charges of censorship. We must, however, sketch in a little background.

In the late twenties the motion pictures, it is quite generally realized now—and was as generally admitted then, even by some of the producers—had just about hit rock bottom as far as their moral tone was concerned. Producers with a concern either for their moral responsibility or for the decline in box-office receipts, or both, as they are not mutually exclusive motives, began to wonder if they ought not adopt a method of regulating themselves. In 1930 there appeared a Production Code of the motion-picture industry, voluntarily subscribed to by all the major companies. Between that date and 1934 the Code was subjected to many reworkings, additions, and subtractions, until a digest of the original Code came in this later year to be known simply as "The Code."[4]

[3] See p. 150 for a reference to Father Facey's unpublished thesis. The material contained in it would amply live up to the qualities here mentioned.

[4] A detailed account of the origin of the Code, its varying fortunes, the misunderstandings about it, and many other interesting details

By 1933 the original ideas behind the Code and a large part of its effectiveness had been lost. The Catholic bishops of the United States, gathered at their annual meeting in November 1933, determined to create a body whose function would be to arouse Catholic opinion against the low moral tone of the films. The first effect of the campaign to alert public opinion was that the motion-picture producers were recalled to the sense of responsibility they had apparently acknowledged in 1930. A Production Code Administration was set up in Hollywood, under the direction of Joseph I. Breen, who for twenty years was to guide the department of the Motion Picture Association which deals directly with producers in administering and applying the freely accepted provisions of the Code. The impression is perhaps unwittingly created by those who view the Code as an infringement of freedom of expression that the motion-picture producers accepted the Code only with the utmost reluctance and would today throw off its restrictions if only they did not fear the wrath of the Catholic Church and especially a concerted drive by the Legion of Decency to force them to submit to the unwelcome reticence. To this we can reply in no better way than to quote Mr. Martin Quigley, who speaks from intimate contact with the industry over three decades. Mr. Quigley flatly states:

"Happily, through experience with it in operation and with its results, the leaders of the motion-picture industry have come to regard [the Code] as an accepted institution of American film production. It has the firm support of the principal industry executives, both in Hollywood and in New York. In fact, the Code as it now stands enjoys such a high degree of determined and even aggressive support that proposals for remedying obvious deficiencies, omissions and confusions . . . have met only with stony-faced disinterest.

"The high measure of executive support which the Code now enjoys is gratifying. It uniquely represents a frank acceptance of moral accountability which is without parallel in

---

will be found in *America*, March 10, 1956, pp. 630–32, "The Motion-Picture Production Code," by Martin J. Quigley. Mr. Quigley was one of the original drafters of the Code and has been a valued consultant at every redrafting and revision.

a commercial field. In all history there is no like instance in the sphere of theatrical entertainment. All this is very good. But it would be even better if those who control its destiny did not seem to view it somewhat as an occult and mysterious formula whose useful spell would disappear in a flash if one jot or tittle were altered."[5]

The support Mr. Quigley claimed for the Code on the part of producers in 1956 is still strong at the present writing. The Catholic bishops of the United States adverted to it obliquely in their statement of November 24, 1960, in which the largely waning moral standard of motion pictures for the preceding year was deplored. The Bishops' Committee on Motion Pictures, Radio and Television, speaking for the entire U.S. hierarchy, noting that "the increased emphasis which films are placing upon unhealthy sex and brutal violence has aroused the deep social concern of religious leaders of all faiths, of public officials, and of respected critics and journalists in the secular and religious press," goes on to state: "Not insignificant has been the insistent cry, *heard within the very ranks of the motion-picture industry itself* [emphasis added], for a reform and for a return to the letter and spirit of the Production Code. We hope that these cries will not fall on deaf ears, for the Code can be and should be a bastion of strength for the industry against morally and socially irresponsible producers and exhibitors who, if unchecked, will feed and pander to the baser instincts of the public."

It is significant and instructive to look back to those early days of the Legion—which many who oppose its work never do—to discover the principles and the spirit with which it undertook its crusade. There was a determined stand from the very start to disassociate the Legion from all forces of political censorship; the Legion eschewed any attempt to use the powers of the state to strengthen its arm. On March 17, 1936, Reverend Joseph A. Daly, then the executive director of the

[5] *America, loc. cit.,* p. 631–32. Mr. Quigley's references to changes in the Code were occasioned by the projected revisions then under discussion. The revised version of the Code was published in 1956 and met with almost universal approval in Catholic circles. The Legion of Decency was particularly gratified by the fact that, far from undermining the moral bases for criticism, the revised Code spelled them out more clearly and workably.

Legion, appeared before a congressional committee which was investigating the problem of "block-booking" in the movie industry.[6] Father Daly stated as a basic principle of the Legion the fact that "the Legion does not believe in or offer support to any legislative short cut to a wholesome screen."[7] In corroboration of this statement, Father Daly quoted from a statement (February 26, 1936) of Archbishop John T. McNicholas of Cincinnati, then chairman of the (Catholic) Episcopal Committee on Motion Pictures:

"The Legion of Decency sees in legislative measures not a means of securing a wholesome screen, but rather a grave danger of political censorship. One law may lead to another. The result in all probability will give us a bureaucracy or final court of morals for motion pictures.

"There would be the danger of political appointees interpreting the provisions of the law in a bureaucracy so as to set up moral standards of motion pictures. There would be danger also of these appointees being influenced by political pressure in their interpretations."[8]

Furthermore, since those early days when the Legion came out against federal censorship, the bishops of the United States, in general, have not been in the forefront of active cooperation in the establishment or retention of individual state censorship boards. One very obvious reason for this is that if the Church, which upholds certain moral principles that are not commonly accepted in this country (divorce, birth control, and the like), were to be vigorous in demanding the continuance of state censor boards, it would be open to a veritable flood of attacks that it was trying to impose through the co-operation of legally constituted organs its own morality on the American public at large. One of the best refutations

---

[6] "Block-booking" was a method of distribution to exhibitors, under which the exhibitors got films in a "package deal." An immoral or otherwise objectionable film had to be taken—and presented—for the exhibitor to be able to get other films. This practice was declared unconstitutional by the United States Supreme Court in 1948.

[7] *Hearing before a Subcommittee of the Committee on Interstate and Foreign Commerce, House of Representatives, 74th Congress, Second Session* (Washington: Government Printing Office, 1936), p. 227. The bill being discussed was the Pettengill Bill (H.R. 6472).

[8] *Ibid.*

of the suspicion that the bishops of the United States are trying to effect such an imposition is precisely their general in-
difference to the existence of state censorship. It was exactly
because political censorship, whether federal or state, was
realized to be ineffectual or dangerous, or both, that the Legion was called into being.[9]

This clear emphasis on the non-political aspects of the mus-
tering of public opinion, which was obvious in the early days
of the Legion, still remains the ideology of those who guide
the Legion's work. This emerges with utmost clarity in the
November 1960 statement of the U.S. Catholic hierarchy, to
which I have referred above. At the time this document was
made public, there was much agitation among the motion-
picture industry about the desirability (increasingly dawning
upon the industry precisely because of the mounting wave of
public opinion) of classifying films so as to indicate those not
for the viewing of the young. One who does not know the
spirit of the Legion would undoubtedly think that this was
a golden opportunity for the Bishops' Committee to come
out in strong support for some sort of compulsory classification imposed on the industry by local, state, or federal law.
But far from it; in unequivocal terms the Committee declared:

> Recalling the 1957 statement of the American hierarchy on
> "Censorship" [this is reprinted in full in Appendix E, p.
> 192 sqq.], we wish to remind the industry that the explicitly

---

[9] The problem of state censorship boards is at present writing a
little academic, since only two states (New York and Maryland) still
have effective bodies; there is a good number of municipal censor
boards. With regard to this relationship between the Legion and
state censorship, two Catholic moral theologians have this to say:
"The stronger the Legion the less need there is to rely on governmental censorship. The Legion is not and has no intention of being
a censorship body. But its system of appraisals has had the end result of protecting public morality and raising artistic standards. It
is our belief that in this country the Legion's method of appraisals,
when supported by well-informed public opinion, both Catholic and
non-Catholic, is a more effective instrument than government censorship enforced by law." (John C. Ford, S.J., and Gerald Kelly,
S.J., "The Legion of Decency," in *Theological Studies* [Woodstock,
Md.], September 1957, p. 387–433.)

stated Catholic preference is for self-regulation on the part of the industry with minimum legal controls. Legislative restrictions either by the municipal or state or federal governments will not be demanded by the public if the industry sets its own house in order. In this connection we set forth certain reasonable proposals which could contribute to a return to responsible production and exhibition:

1. Some system must be devised by the industry to safeguard young and impressionable minds from that subject matter and treatment in films which they are not yet mature enough to assimilate [see, in this connection, the remarks on pp. 98–99 on the Legion's new (1957) classifications designed to deal with the adolescent audience]. A system of self-classification of films by the industry cannot be lightly disregarded.

2. Although adult-oriented production is not only a legitimate but even a necessary maturation of the motion-picture medium, such production must conform to the spirit of the Production Code. As long as the Code is sincerely and intelligently applied, it is specious and irresponsible to argue that film classification would lead to "adulterous" production by the organized industry.

The statement then goes on to recommend proper restraint in the advertising of films and a determination on the part of exhibitors to show only those films that have received the Code's seal of approval.

At the same Congressional hearing in 1936, Father Daly went on to spell out the specific function of the Legion of Decency:

"The Legion has one clear, simple objective—to insure for the public, as legitimate recreation, a wholesome screen against which there can be no objections on moral grounds. Its strongest weapon has been an aroused public opinion, and public opinion will continue to be the most effectual safeguard against salacious motion pictures. The Legion of Decency regards public opinion as a much safer guide than would be any regulations made by political appointees in a Federal agency. . . .

"Producers have invited reasonable and constructive criticism, with much benefit morally to the public which seeks entertainment in motion pictures.

"Since there has been a marked improvement in the moral tone of pictures, effected through public opinion, it seems reasonable to let the good work go on. The Legion of Decency will continue to be vigilant and to urge that all groups maintain an active interest in the moral significance of the motion pictures."[10]

As a commentary on the work of the Legion in those initial years, Samuel B. Pettengill, congressman from Indiana and chairman of the subcommittee, had this to say: "Father Daly, I want to say to you and to the bishops for whom you speak, that I congratulate you and them . . . upon the development of public opinion which you have contributed to the solution of this problem. I think it is one of the most notable contributions to public life in America in recent years."[11]

Now it is true that the public opinion to which the Legion appeals operates in the concrete when Catholics hearken to the listings of the Legion and stay away from pictures that are, in whatever degree, condemned. This abstention on the part of Catholics constitutes, if one insists on using the word, a boycott, and a boycott inevitably involves a loss of revenue. A movie producer or a theatre owner, faced with such a loss, will understandably feel that he is being subjected to economic threat or pressure. It must be admitted, as well, that when the U.S. Catholic hierarchy announced the launching of the Legion of Decency campaign, some bishops made explicit use of the word "boycott" or "censorship."[12]

The overwhelming emphasis, however, was always of the force of public opinion, which was to be galvanized and stimulated, but not dragooned, through a concerted effort by Catholics for Catholics. The specific form this public opinion took at the very beginning was the Legion of Decency Pledge, which,

10 *Ibid.*, p. 228.

11 *Ibid.*, p. 232.

12 Pastoral letters of some fourteen U.S. prelates announcing the inauguration of the campaign may be consulted in the *Catholic Mind*, August 8, 1934, pp. 281–300, and September 8, 1934, pp. 321–40.

as approved by the Episcopal Committee on Motion Pictures, ran as follows:

"I wish to join the Legion of Decency, which condemns vile and unwholesome moving pictures. I unite with all who protest against them as a grave menace to youth, to home life, to country and to religion.

"I condemn absolutely those salacious motion pictures, which, with other degrading agencies, are corrupting public morals and promoting a sex mania in our land.

"I shall do all that I can to arouse public opinion against the portrayal of vice as a normal condition of affairs, and against depicting criminals of any class as heroes and heroines, presenting their filthy philosophy of life as something acceptable to decent men and women.

"I unite with all who condemn the display of suggestive advertisements on billboards, at theatre entrances, and the favorable notices given to immoral motion pictures.

"Considering these evils, I hereby promise to remain away from all motion pictures except those which do not offend decency and Christian morality. I promise further to secure as many members as possible for the Legion of Decency.

"I make this protest in a spirit of self-respect and with the conviction that the American public does not demand filthy pictures, but clean entertainment and educational features."[13]

This pledge has been simplified over the years and in 1958 was revised to run less rhetorically, perhaps, but no less forthrightly:

"I condemn indecent and immoral motion pictures, and those which glorify crime or criminals.

"I promise to do all that I can to strengthen public opinion against the production of indecent and immoral films, and to unite with all who protest against them.

"I acknowledge my obligation to form a right conscience about pictures that are dangerous to my moral life. As a member of the Legion of Decency, I pledge myself to remain away from them. I promise, further, to stay away altogether from places of amusement which show them as a matter of policy."

[13] *Catholic Mind,* August 8, 1934, pp. 281–82.

Further, in 1960 the pledge was rephrased so as to emphasize the idea of promoting the good in motion pictures (instead of merely condemning the bad) and to stress the fact that these promises are resolutions, and not in any sense an "oath." This newest form of the pledge has been at present writing adopted in some N.Y. dioceses:

I promise to promote by word and deed what is morally and artistically good in motion-picture entertainment.

I promise to discourage indecent, immoral, and unwholesome motion pictures especially by my good example and always in a responsible and civic-minded manner.

I promise to guide those under my care and influence in their choice of motion pictures that are morally and culturally inspiring.

I promise not to co-operate by my patronage with theatres which regularly show objectionable films.

I promise as a member of the Legion of Decency to acquaint myself with its aims, to consult its classifications, and to unite with all men of good will in promoting high and noble standards in motion-picture entertainment.

I freely make these solemn resolutions to the honor of God for the good of my soul and for the welfare of my country. Amen.

The essential thing to be remembered about this pledge in any of its forms, particularly by Catholics, but specifically here by those who feel that the Legion is regimenting American minds, has been expressed very well by Reverend John C. Ford, S.J., professor of moral theology at Weston College, Weston, Massachusetts. Writing on the subject of "Moral Evaluation of Films by the Legion of Decency," Father Ford states:

"One of the most attractive features of the Legion of Decency has been the voluntary character of the pledge which Catholics make to support it. The very thing that gives its spiritual life and supernatural inspiration is the fact that it does not of itself impose obligations under pain of sin. When the people stand up in church to renew their pledge, they do it with a sense of Christian heroism and dedication precisely because they are doing something they do not have to do;

because they are surrendering for the love of God their liberty and their pleasure, at least in some degree."[14]

Catholics are offered the opportunity to take this pledge every year on the Sunday after the Feast of the Immaculate Conception (December 8), when it is read to them from the pulpits of their parish churches. It is worth pointing out that the pledge is couched in general terms and actually does no more than specify and recall an obligation that Catholics (and indeed any Christians) would be faced with, even if there were no Legion of Decency—the obligation, namely, not to attend motion pictures or any other type of entertainment that is offensive to Christian morality.

The work of the U. S. National Legion of Decency was canonized, as it were, by the encyclical *Vigilanti Cura* ("In following with vigilant eye," the first phrase of the document), of Pope Piux XI, issued on June 29, 1936. In it His Holiness lauds the "excellent experiment" inaugurated by the American hierarchy and calls on the bishops of the Catholic world to emulate the work of the Legion. It is to the point to recall that the Pope adverted to the fact that "economic threat" or "pressure" was inseparable from any widespread Catholic abstention from such films. This, however, he indicated, was what we may call a by-product, for the whole Legion crusade "had far from it the thought of doing damage to the motion-picture industry . . . nor have financial investments in the industry suffered. . . . Those who stayed away from the motion-picture theatre because it outraged morality are patronizing it, now that they are able to enjoy clean films which are not offensive to good morals or dangerous to Christian virtue."[15]

Another key papal document which must be consulted in any discussion of the moral responsibility of the communica-

[14] This is one of the unpublished documents in the files of the Legion of Decency office in New York. I am forced to a twofold observation: the Legion's public-relation activities should make such statements widely available to the Catholic and non-Catholic public alike; the lack of such efficiency gives the lie to those who maintain that the Legion is a pressure group.

[15] The encyclical may be consulted in the *Catholic Mind*, August 8, 1936, pp. 305–17.

tion media is the encyclical *Miranda Prorsus* ("Remarkable Inventions") of Pope Pius XII (September 8, 1957). It is a very long encyclical, running to some thirteen thousand words, which discusses thoroughly the marvelous opportunities for education and proper entertainment enjoyed by the films, radio, and television, and recalls to all concerned the staggering responsibilities that are also entailed. The Pope calls for the strengthening of national Catholic offices which will be devoted to engaging public opinion in a concerted effort to raise moral standards. It is noteworthy how insistent the Pope is on the "mutual co-operation" necessary for such improvement; some, of course, will think that Pius XII is also calling for wider "censorship," but the fair-minded reader of the encyclical will not fail to hear the theme that public opinion can shape moral standards for the common good. *Vigilanti Cura* and *Miranda Prorsus*, read in conjunction, provide a magnificent statement of the confidence that exists in papal thinking that social problems *can* be solved if men of good will will work together for the common good.[16]

This same idea is predominant, too, in the November 16, 1957, statement of the U.S. Catholic hierarchy. The joint statement was rather sensationally headlined in the secular press as being a declaration of all-out war on obscenity; it was, rather, a very complete and reasoned statement on the proper functions of censorship in a pluralistic society. Since the official statement deals with the very subject that this book treats, and since it summarizes so pithily what I have dealt with more discursively in these pages, it seems good to include the statement among the appendices.

To return to a consideration of *Vigilanti Cura*: this authoritative papal pronouncement sheds light on the matter of suspected Catholic "regimentation" of approach to moral questions as they arise in motion pictures. The Pope states that it is ideally desirable that a single classification of the moral standards of pictures should be drawn up for the whole

---

[16] The latest Papal pronouncement on the whole subject is the encyclical *Boni Pastoris* ("The duty of a good pastor"), by John XXIII (February 22, 1959; the complete text is given in the *Catholic Mind*, July–August 1959, pp. 367–71), which reaffirms the teaching of *Miranda Prorsus*.

world, "since all live under the same moral laws." But the Pope is a realist, too (as all moralists have to be), and he goes on:

"Since, however, there is here a question of pictures which interest all classes of society, the great and the humble, the learned and the unlettered, the judgment passed upon the film cannot be the same in each case in all respects.

"Indeed, circumstances, usages and forms vary from country to country, so that it does not seem practical to have a list [of morally evaluated films] for all the world."[17]

This simple observation of Pius XI gives the clear reason why there is no hard and fast "Catholic line" that covers with adamantine precision all possible cases. One of the elements that determines the morality of human acts is the element of the circumstances. Indecent exposure, to take an example, is always and everywhere against the very basis of morality. But what is indecent exposure? In the South Sea isles exposed bosoms are standard dress, may we say, but not on Fifth Avenue. But even in the South Sea islands, custom and circumstances will not tolerate *all* physical exposure. It is most instructive, in this connection, to see that the Legion of Decency gave in 1957 an A-2 rating (morally unobjectionable for adults) to *The Lost Continent*, a film in which native marriage customs in Borneo focused the camera for considerable footage on undraped female torsos. In the context—that of a very reverent documentary film—the semi-nudity was to-

---

[17] *Ibid.*, p. 315. A most instructive treatment of the cultural differences that can and do exist under Catholic film ratings, especially abroad, is given in the September 28 issue of *America*, "Catholic Film Work in Europe," by Erik von Kuehnelt-Leddihn, pp. 670–72. The author remarks: "We must never forget that the problem of classifying films has no simple solution. One cannot place the age-groups or the generations on the same psychological level. People of different nations, or of different regions within a nation, different native intelligence or different experience, cannot all be approached in the same way. . . . Yet we are living in an age that would like to standardize personality and to regard human beings as interchangeable and 'equal' ciphers. The Catholic film leagues [this has special reference to groups abroad, but the general truth applies to the Legion here as well] know this only too well; and therefore they insinuate rather than openly express educational differences in their classifications."

tally and properly in keeping. What the Legion had, and quite properly, to say was that the advertisement for the film gave a totally wrong and (especially for the young) seductive accent.

This procedure of giving moral classification to motion pictures is the core feature of the Legion's operations and is, obviously, a matter of assessment, not of censorship. A discussion of the classifications is necessary here to round out our sketch of the Legion's history. A further problem is occasioned by the classifications: the problem of the moral responsibility of Catholics to inform themselves of the classifications of individual films and to shape their attendance accordingly. This will be adverted to somewhat later.

From the very beginning of the Legion's work, the classification of films took very nearly the form that was operative into 1957. Here are the classifications and their interpretations under which the Legion worked until December 1957:

A-1: *Morally Unobjectionable for General Patronage.*
These films are considered to contain no material which would be morally dangerous to the average motion-picture audience, adults and children alike.

A-2: *Morally Unobjectionable for Adults.*
These are films which in themselves are morally harmless but which, because of subject-matter or treatment, require maturity and experience if one is to witness them without danger of moral harm. While no definite age limit can be established for this group, the judgment of parents, pastors and teachers would be helpful in determining the decision in individual cases.

B: *Morally Objectionable in Part for All.*
Films in this category are considered to contain elements dangerous to Christian morals or moral standards.

C: *Condemned.*
Condemned films are considered to be those which, because of theme or treatment, have been described by the Holy Father as "positively bad."

Separate Classification.
This is given to certain films which, while not morally offensive, require some analysis and explanation as a protection

to the uninformed against wrong interpretations and false conclusions.

In December 1957, however, the Legion revised the classifications for reasons that will be indicated further on. Now the moral classifications read as follows:

A-1: Morally Unobjectionable for General Patronage.
A-2: Morally Unobjectionable for *Adults* and *Adolescents*.
A-3: Morally Unobjectionable for *Adults*.
B: Morally Objectionable in Part for *All*.
C: Condemned.

The Legion gave the following reasons for the new classifications:

"(a) The Legion recognizes that in connection with motion-picture attendance the average adolescent of our day will not infrequently consider himself more than a child and hence will seek pictures with more adult content and orientation. In keeping with the sound principles of modern Catholic educational psychology, it seems desirable that the Legion aid the adolescent in this quest for more mature movie-subjects and thereby contribute to his intellectual and emotional maturation. To this end the new A-2 classification has been adopted; it is hoped that this classification, while providing the necessary reasonable moral controls upon the adolescent, will at the same time aid him in his 'growing up.'

"(b) The A-3 classification is an attempt on the part of the Legion to provide for truly adult subject matter in entertainment motion pictures, provided that the themes in question and their treatment be consonant with the moral law and with traditionally-accepted moral standards.

"(c) Although the B and C classifications remain unchanged, it is to be recognized that the new triple A classification is intended also to strengthen the meaning of the B category. Henceforth, there will be no doubt that a B film is one adjudged to contain material which in itself or in its offensive treatment is contrary to traditional morality and constitutes a threat not only to the personal spiritual life of even an adult viewer, but also to the moral behavior-patterns which condition public morality. Catholic people are urged to refrain from attendance at all B pictures, not only for the sake of their own consciences, but also in the interest of promoting the common good."

It may be well to remark that this latest development in the work of the Legion is a definite move toward more positive attitudes; it underlines, too, the fact that the work of the Legion is a living work: it strives to adapt moral evaluations to concrete circumstances and to foster the intellectual and moral growth of the moviegoer. In so far as this is aimed at and achieved, the Legion again manifests that it is not a censorship agency; censorship pure and simple is never interested in more than a negative result. Furthermore, since 1958 the Legion has become more and more concerned with an even more positive approach. Without ever losing sight of the fact that its prime mandate is to categorize films according to moral standards, the Legion has moved into the admittedly somewhat limited field of striving to combat the bad by commending the good. This is indicated in the opening phrase of the latest version of the pledge (see p. 93), wherein the promise is made to promote what is "artistically" good. In addition, from time to time, the Legion has singled out pictures for positive recommendation as morally and artistically endorsed for general—that is, family—viewing. This accent on the positive has gone to such films as *The Inn of the Sixth Happiness*, *Ben Hur*, *Embezzled Heaven*, *Conspiracy of Hearts*, and *The Nun's Story*; it is safe to say that the Legion is more aware today than it ever was in the past that this positive approach is not merely a matter of good public relations with the film industry but, more important, constitutes an affirmative attitude to the good that is to be found in sound art and a reaffirmation of the Catholic principles on this matter as stated in *Miranda Prorsus* and *Boni Pastoris*.

The question of the obligation of Catholics to know and follow the Legion's ratings need not detain us long, for the simple reason that it is not germane to the matter of this book. We are not treating precisely the control of films as it affects Catholics, but rather Catholic attitudes on control as they fit into the cultural life of the country. However, a few remarks on the subject cannot be entirely avoided, if only for the historical record.

The older A-1 and A-2 classifications posed no moral problem for Catholics, especially if what the Legion had to say about "adulthood" was kept in mind:

"The term adulthood, in its complete sense, does not necessarily depend upon age. Age, of course, constitutes a measure of approximate determination. Adulthood, in its complete sense, involves a certain amount of maturity—physical, emotional, mental and spiritual.

"One should hesitate to become so specific as to mention a definite age at which, in all cases, childhood and adolescence cease and adulthood begins.

"It is necessary to be familiar with the indicators and factors which interpose themselves, viz., physical age; scholastic grade and grading; capacity to perceive, face, solve or adjust to the various problems of life and existence; degree of possession of ideas, standards and motivations; accessibility, competence and effectiveness of parental, pedagogical and religious guidance; domestic, social and economic environment—et cetera.

"Parents, clergymen and teachers having in their care and charge children and adolescents are in particularly advantageous positions to judge the time of the inception of adulthood."

There was practical consensus among Catholic moral theologians that pictures rated C (condemned) were of their very nature such as to constitute a definite moral danger to the "average" or "normal" Catholic. Here again we have to hark back to the norms of Canon Law and the obligations of positive law. Any individual Catholic may feel sure that such-and-such a C picture would cause him no harm, but the caution issued by the Legion in the very act of condemning ought to be respected, keeping in mind the wise commentary of St. Thomas that "to make a rule to fit every case is impossible. Legislators have to attend to what happens in the majority of cases and should frame their laws accordingly."[18] No sincere Catholic ought knowingly view a C picture without a properly justifying reason, such, for instance, as the professional necessity of a reviewer for the Legion. If an individual Catholic knows that a certain C picture will not harm his moral stand-

[18] *Summa Theologica*, 2a–2ae, cxx, 1.

ards and that he can see it without creating scandal, he will not sin against, let us say, the sixth commandment if he sees it; he may sin against the virtue of prudence in flouting presumably informed advice from the Legion or against obedience to legitimate ecclesiastical authority, if his bishop, for instance, has issued a specific condemnation of the film.

It was the B (morally objectionable in part for all) rating that occasioned some controversy. Suffice it to say that some moral theologians took a more strict view as to the obligation of Catholics to stay away from B films; other moralists were somewhat more lenient. Quite an extensive literature developed around the debate, but to follow all the ramifications of the debate would carry us too far into a domestic problem.[19]

Much of the divergence between the more "liberal" and the more "strict" view on the B classification has now been eliminated by the new classifications. By giving adolescent film-viewers a definite recognition, the Legion has automatically "strengthened" the B classification: that is to say, the moral objections against such films are now more weighty and obvious, and the corresponding obligation of Catholics to avoid them are stronger.

But, to avoid the morally objectionable films and to support the morally and artistically good ones, the Catholic public must be informed. And so, in the November 1960 statement of the U.S. bishops the obligation of parents is strongly adverted to:

> Priests and educators are exhorted . . . in accordance with the directives of the Holy See, to convince the faith-

19 The reader may be referred to a booklet, "The Legion of Decency," by Avery Dulles, S.J., America Press, 1956 (reprinted from *America*, June 2, 1956, pp. 240–42), which provides one of the most comprehensive statements available and which, at the same time, is marked by a "liberal" tone. Stricter interpretations of the B classification may be found in various articles by Father Connell, such as the one in the April 1946 issue of the *American Ecclesiastical Review*. Father Connell has not modified his rigid stand in later years. A later treatment, which is even more comprehensive than that of Father Dulles, is available in the article in *Theological Studies* referred to above. It goes into great detail on such matters as the weight of obligation to be attached to papal and episcopal statements and

ful of the prudent necessity of consulting the Legion's classifications before attendance at any motion picture.

Parents particularly must be reminded that they are seriously delinquent in the fulfilment of their parental duties if they permit their children to attend films not approved for them. Indeed, indiscriminate attendance at any film by young or old can only manifest a pathetic disregard for good moral and artistic taste.

It sheds light on the widespread social concern about films, and is somewhat amusing, to see how these various aspects of the Legion are now being given some pats on the back. Consider, for instance, an editorial in *Life* magazine titled "Bluer Movies, Not-So-Blue Noses" (December 5, 1960). Reporting the Legion's findings that in 1960 the percentage of "objectionable" films has risen to 24 per cent, as against 14 per cent for 1959, and remarking that "public censorship" has proved generally inoperative, mainly because it has been "kidded out of office in most states," the editorial continues:

> Private censorship is quite another matter. The freer the screen and the more venturesome the producers, the more responsibility devolves on citizens to do their own censoring, especially parents. Every parent is the best qualified censor for his family. He can't preview everything showing, but he can keep pretty good tabs by reading the ads, the reviews, and maybe a guidance list or two. The Legion of Decency's own classifications, available in all Catholic churches, is [*sic!*] a useful adjunct to the discharge of this parental duty. . . . The most effective boycott in the long run is the silent boycott of vigilant parents. The family is the most appropriate organ of censorship in our society. It seems about time for more parents to go to work at this part of their job.

It may seem overly optimistic, perhaps, but such an editorial in a mass-circulation journal, mirroring as it does a wide discontent with the present status of the films, seems to presage a return to the general approval given to the work of the

kindred matters that would take us into discussion not germane to the purposes of this book.

Legion in its earlier days, a much overlooked historical and sociological fact I shall have occasion to dwell on later in the chapter on "'Pressure Groups,' Boycott, and Co-operation."

A further point. Catholics themselves betray that they do not really appreciate the purposes of the Legion when they question how grave the obligation is or is not to follow the Legion's classifications. True, this question does inevitably arise, but the prime purpose of the Legion is not concerned with a matter of obligation; among Catholics as well as in the body of U.S. citizens, the capital goal of the Legion is the arousal of public opinion—if we may repeat that phrase *ad nauseam*. Catholics should avoid B and C pictures, not precisely because such films constitute an immediate danger to moral life, but because the Catholic body is concerned to work with the Legion to create a *moral atmosphere* wherein such pictures will become fewer and fewer.

How does the Legion actually arrive at the specific classification of a particular film? To answer this question it seems best to let one answer who has been at the head of the review work of the Legion for several decades. Again, it is ardently to be wished that material of this type were readily available to the general public, and especially to the more vociferous critics of the Legion. The following remarks were made by Mrs. James F. Looram, chairman of the Motion Picture Department of the International Confederation of Catholic Alumnae, at the twentieth convention of the IFCA held at St. Paul on August 26, 1955. The IFCA has supplied the Legion's reviewing staff from the very start.

"First of all, the reviewer, as a graduate of our Catholic academies and colleges, brings to her work that background of Catholic ethics and philosophy which is an essential prerequisite for her task.

"Our religion does not proscribe entertainment. St. Thomas Aquinas says that entertainment is a right of human nature which is so constituted that it needs diversion and recreation. That the contemporary Church has preserved the attitude of St. Thomas towards entertainment is revealed in the words of Pius XI:

"'Recreation in its manifold variety has become a necessity of people who labor under the fatiguing conditions of modern industry.' . . . 'With its magnificent power, the screen can and must be a light and a positive guide to what is good.'

"A very important qualification, therefore, of a reviewer is her appreciation of wholesome motion picture entertainment. (An open mind is most essential.) The reviewer's yardstick is *traditional* standards of morality upon which the sanctification of the individual, the sacredness of the home and ethical foundation of civilization necessarily depend.

"The members of the review group are responsibly chosen because of their specific qualifications and special qualifications and special ability in applying principles of objective morality to entertainment motion pictures. Under the guidance of experts in the field of morality and decency, they continue their training for many years before they are considered skilled reviewers. This training is given under the guidance and counsel of priests of the Legion's executive staff and others.

"Recruits must pass through a six-months period of training. During this time they attend weekly previews and at the end of the screening a discussion is led by one of the veteran members. Individual opinions are solicited, reasons for different ratings given by the Legion are explained and applications made to particular points raised by the film they have just seen. The veteran reviewers make their reports privately and separately. They send in a written ballot with a number of questions answered and a number of definite reasons given for a certain classification.

"At the regular monthly meetings of the entire reviewing group, the clergy from the National Legion Office and the Chairman of the Motion Picture Department discuss with the reviewers pictures which have provoked differences of opinion, or have offered some special difficulty.

"Pictures which have been condemned by the reviewers or have raised serious question among them are submitted to the Consultors Committee of the Legion of Decency. The consultors group is made up of twenty Catholic laymen and clergymen. Some of these gentlemen are canon lawyers, some are doctors, dentists, teachers and labor leaders. They were selected as representatives of a cross section of society rather than for any influence or prestige they might possess in the group from which they come. [Since this address was delivered by Mrs. Looram, the structure of the regular review board, and especially the size and the personnel of the board of consultants, has been considerably modified. In addition to the members of the IFCA, the regular review staff now comprises priests, with emphasis on those who are experienced in some aspects of sociology, such as work with the young, and laymen who are professional critics, engaged in the communications media, or otherwise trained to evaluate the films. In addition, the board of consultants, which is called upon much more frequently now, and not merely when a picture has been condemned or raised serious questions, numbers one hundred, drawn from all walks of life.]

"To acquire the necessary set of judicial norms for carrying on their tasks, the IFCA reviewers read two treatises: *How to Judge the Morality of Motion Pictures* and *The Morals of the Screen* and, most important, *Vigilanti Cura.*

"They also read Mr. Martin J. Quigley's book, *Decency in Motion Pictures,* which provides the reviewers with the historical background of the conflict which led to their activity and includes the text of the Production Code. The Code gives the reviewers a statement of what to expect from Hollywood films. (Unfortunately of late, these expectations are not always realized.)

"*How to Judge the Morality of Motion Pictures* describes itself as 'a popular guide to right standards in motion-picture entertainment, authorized by the Episcopal Committee on Motion Pictures for the Legion of Decency.' Its eight pages summarily set forth the moral significance and influence of movies, the purpose of the Legion of Decency, the nature of the Production Code, the Legion's attitude towards the Code, what should and should not be portrayed in the movies and six examples of the objectionable types of pictures. The general thesis of the pamphlet is that the Legion, while it condemns obscenity, salaciousness and suggestiveness, is principally concerned with films which present false moral standards which in turn lower traditional morality.

"The reviewer sees four to eight feature films a week. Within twenty-four hours after reviewing a film she sends in her written four-page analysis of it. With the artistic, enter-

tainment and technical value of the film, the reviewer is *not*
concerned. [This statement must now be viewed in the light
of the newer approach as sketched on p. 99.] She checks on
the morality of the theme, the decency or indecency of treatment. She notes, in cases of the portrayal of evil, whether
there are any voices of morality to make articulate the moral
principles involved in the issue being dramatized.

"The *theme* of a movie is what largely determines its morality. Every well-constructed film can be summarized in a
question and an answer concerning the leading character. We
ought to be able to say that the movie 'is about a person who
is faced with this or that problem and does this or that about
it.'

"It is the answer given rather than the problem presented
that constitutes the morality of the theme as such. If it were
not for this, very few real dilemmas of life could be presented
at all, and no stories of repentance after wrongdoing.

"In cases where the decision itself is immoral, the writer
may still have a moral theme if he created dislike instead of
sympathy for the leading character, and shows how the false
decision leads to tragedy and retribution, such as in *Macbeth*.

"The reviewer notes whether there is reform, regeneration,
punishment, retribution: in other words—adequate moral
compensation. She answers such questions as: 'Is the film contrary to or in consonance with Christian and traditional standards of morality?'

"She is careful to check if the film treats marriage lightly,
if it reflects the acceptability of divorce, if it is suggestive in
sequence, costuming and dialog; if suicide is shown whether it
is presented as justified or as plot solution or if it is presented
as double effect or under the guise of heroism. She must be
meticulously careful to note if sin is presented as a mistake
or as a shameful transgression.

"These and many other problems, if present in the film, are
analyzed objectively by the reviewer whose prime qualification is not that of being a super-sifter of cinema sin, but of
applying her alert and intelligent understanding of what constitutes acceptable entertainment according to standards of
Christian morality.

"Sin must always be shown for what it is, not a mistake but

a shameful transgression. Crime is not an error of frailty but the breaking of the law. Wrong is not pleasant but painful, not heroic but cowardly, not profitable but detrimental, not plausible but deserving of condemnation.

"Of course, our reviewers are not infallible. Until the baseball umpire calls all the plays to the satisfaction of everyone on the teams and in the stands, we cannot expect to be infallible for, like the umpire, we are human.

"It is only natural that there will be a variance of receptivity to certain films. In the matter of costuming and suggestiveness, whether in dance, dialog, or situations, we often have a divided opinion among our reviewers. However, the type and nature of the film, together with the intentions and motivations of the director, are judged. Many times a determining factor is the time, place and circumstances in which the story content is developed. The over-all good effect or positive values in the film can greatly minimize the immoral effect of certain sequences.

"The reviewer knows that certainly the prerogative of the screen is to hold up a mirror to the realities of life. Conflict between evil and good is the very life-blood of the living drama but to distort one by making it appear desirable, or the other by implying that it is inconsequential, demoralizes human thinking and degenerates dramatic art."

Thus Mrs. Looram's explanation of how the Legion's reviewing staff judges an individual film. This is the material that is then passed along to the Legion's executive secretary and his assistant, both of whom are priests and who, as a general rule, have also seen the film being voted on. Their function is to appraise the reviewers' judgments and to assign to the many votes a qualitative analysis. It is not a mere matter of totting up the number of votes that a film should be classified, let us say, B or C, but a matter of judging the cogency, the maturity, the balance and judiciousness of the total reaction of the reviewing staff. Only after this considerate judgment is the classification finally determined upon.

After the films have been reviewed and classified, the ratings are publicized among the Catholic body in various ways: through the Catholic press, in sermons, at school assemblies and talks, and so on, so that Catholics at large may be informed of what is acceptable and what objectionable film entertainment. This is the major function of the Legion; a secondary but important activity, which occurs only from time to time, consists in conferences with producers at which the Legion's objections are explained and argument is made for the elimination of the grounds upon which the objections are based. It should be pointed out that such conferences are *always* initiated by the producers, never by the Legion.

In each diocese there is a local director of the Legion, appointed by the bishop, who "puts into operation the ideals and standards of the National Office." This feature of the Legion's work needs some clarification in the public mind. According to Canon Law, each bishop is the supreme spiritual authority in his own diocese; hence the local bishop may go farther, if he feels there is a particular need because of local circumstances, in applying sanctions against a particular picture or, indeed, a theatre. This was done recently (in March 1957), for instance, in the diocese of Albany, where the bishop forbade Catholics to attend for a period of six months a theatre that had shown the C-rated film, *Baby Doll*. This is, indeed, a type of punitive boycott and is rather rare in the history of the Legion. Some Catholic opinion might debate its public-relations value in these days when Catholic-Protestant tensions are so much in the wind; but no one—certainly no informed Catholic—can question the authority of a local bishop to act in such a way.

Furthermore, this freedom of action enjoyed by the local bishops has its bearing, which is little thought of, in the matter of supposed Catholic censorship. Though the Legion of Decency is an organ of the corporate Catholic hierarchy in the United States, it has no jurisdictional function; it is, to repeat, an agency of information and guidance; it issues no orders to the local bishops. To be sure, the American hierarchy accepts and even accents the ratings given by the Legion, in pastoral letters, in sermons, and so on; the bishops agree on the one list of ratings as prepared by the Legion and, though a bishop may be more stringent on a particular film because of local circumstances, he may not, according to the directives of *Vigilanti Cura*, apply a less strict rating. Nevertheless, the Legion is not an instrument of central regimentation, even for

Catholics, and infinitely less for the American public at large. As we shall be able to point out even more effectively when we take up the NODL, here in the case of the Legion, those who dislike its principles and practices give it credit (if that is the word) for being much more tightly organized, much more at the steering wheel than it actually is or wishes to be.

From this account of the rise and present functioning of the Legion, we may be in a position to answer the question: Does the activity of the Legion constitute censorship? A related question is: If the Legion's work *is* censorship, is it of a type that is repellent to Americans?

To answer the first question we have to recall the distinction dwelt upon in the first section of this book: prior censorship (*censura praevia,* in the terms of Canon Law) and subsequent suppression or control (*censura repressiva*). Prior censorship—that is, suppression of a film or book before release to the general public—is what is especially deprecated by those who combat censorship. As regards the films, the trend in recent Supreme Court decisions and in various state enactments is definitely against prior censorship. I say trend, for it is not true that *all* prior censorship of *all* types of films has been declared unconstitutional. Decisions in various state courts have been reversed by the Supreme Court, but always on the ground that the prior censorship (by state review bodies, for instance) was exercised on grounds that could not provide enough legal precision to sustain charges. In the famous *Miracle* case (*Burnstyn* v. *Wilson,* 72 S. Ct. 777), for instance, the Supreme Court "did not hold that in all cases pre-exhibition restraints upon exhibition of motion pictures are unconstitutional."[20] The Court simply declared that the charge that the picture was "sacrilegious" was too vague in our pluralistic society to justify prior censorship or to sustain subsequent criminal prosecution. In the very decision (through a dictum by Mr. Justice Felix Frankfurter), however, it was

[20] Leo Pfeffer, *The Liberties of an American* (Boston: The Beacon Press, 1956), p. 144–45. The author's adequate summary of the film is: "*The Miracle* was a forty-minute Italian-language film relating the tale of a simple ["minded" must be added] peasant girl who is seduced by a bearded stranger she imagines to be St. Joseph and who later gives birth to a baby she believes to have been divinely conceived."

explicitly stated that the Court might "approve a clearly-drawn statute designed and applied to *prevent* [emphasis added] the showing of obscene films." This is a point worth keeping in mind, for we heard it said fairly generally and very imprecisely by the anti-censorship cohorts that prior censorship (or restraint) in general is un-American. This is simply not true. "Neither," says Mr. Pfeffer, continuing his remarks on *The Miracle* case, "are pre-publication restraints on printing in all cases unconstitutional . . . but protection against previous restraint, though not absolutely unlimited, is the rule, not the exception."[21]

The *climate* of legal opinion, however, as we developed above, is against prior censorship, which now, apparently, can be brought into play only when a book or a film is obscene in the recently canonized sense. If such a work is charged simply with being "indecent," "immoral," "sacrilegious," "vulgar," and a host of other dubious epithets, prior restraint will most probably be held to be unconstitutional. Whether or not Catholics, among others, regret this extreme care as shown by our courts, it must be granted that the courts are actually operating, whether they know it or not, in the very spirit of Canon Law (in so far as it deals with obscenity), which, as we have seen, is very careful to limit precisely the boundaries of legislation which restricts human liberty. And practically speaking, it is hard to see what else our courts can do in trying to preserve liberty while protecting morals. The protection the civil law can give to morals is bound to be minimal, as St. Thomas reminds us: "Human law cannot forbid all and everything that is against virtue; it is enough that it forbids deeds against community life; the remainder it tolerates almost as if they were licit, not indeed because they are approved, but because they are not punished."[22]

With this minor digression in mind, let us turn to the activities of the Legion of Decency. The Legion does not exercise prior censorship. The vast, overwhelming number of the films it reviews are already in the pipeline to the general public and will be released, frequently enough before the

[21] *Op. cit.*, p. 145. See the statement of Mr. Justice Frankfurter in the Kingsley case, above, p. 77.
[22] *Summa Theologica*, 2a–2ae, lxxvii, 1 ad 1.

Legion's ratings get to public attention (a situation the Legion tries valiantly to cope with).

But does the Legion exercise repressive censorship, an effort to control the viewing of pictures after they are released? Yes: but only for those to whom it has a delegated authority to speak—to Catholics. If New York's Cardinal Spellman, for instance, in issuing his strong condemnation of *Baby Doll*, saw fit to urge "all decent-minded and patriotic citizens" to join in the Catholic protest, some American citizens who are certainly in their own consciences patriotic and decent-minded might have resented the implied charge, but on what grounds could they have thought that they were being ordered not to see the film?

Of course the Legion is trying to set up a climate of opinion in which Catholics, Protestants, Jews, all men of good will, will feel at home. Of course the Legion would like to see droves of people, Catholics and others, staying away from pictures that are smutty and suggestive and sadistic and vulgar, if not downright indecent. But it works to accomplish such a happy state of affairs through public opinion and moral persuasion. And of course a solidified and active public opinion is going to hurt the movie box offices; here arises the sinister "boycott" and "economic-threat" zombie.

Judge Curtis L. Bok of the Superior Court of Pennsylvania, writing in the *Saturday Review* for July 11, 1953, delivered himself of a remark that is pertinent to this stage of our discussion. The judge is a noted defender of freedom of speech, as well, obviously, as of other freedoms we pride ourselves upon, but in the course of his discussion on "The Duty of Freedom" he said: "Hence I believe in the censorship of the open market rather than of the police station." If the matter is given a little calm and sincere thought, is not that precisely the type of "censorship" the Legion exercises—the "censorship of the open market"? Films get produced and get shown; they take their chances. A group of Catholics get together and say, "We thought you would offer us bread and you gave us a brick; we don't like bricks for a diet; we'll have nothing to do with such films." Where is the "censorship"; where the "economic threat"? If our non-Catholic friends say, "Yes, but you Catholics were dragooned into such a statement," well, that is a problem for Catholics to handle for themselves. Meanwhile we like the "censorship of the open market," and it strikes us that any effort to suppress the Legion—and what are charges that it is un-American, undemocratic, but attempts to suppress through the social pressures of ridicule, disdain, and contempt?—is an attempt to shut off the channels of free opinion and debate that make for a socially, intellectually, and morally stronger America.

CHAPTER III

The National Office for Decent Literature

When we turn to an examination of the goal and work of the NODL, the problem posed by Catholic "censorship" activities gets considerably more complicated. One clear reason for this is that we are now in the field of the printed word. It is true that recent Supreme Court decisions have accorded to motion pictures the same constitutional safeguards of freedom that the press has long and traditionally enjoyed, having reversed a 1915 ruling that motion pictures are "mere" entertainment. Still, it is true that the "silver screen," no matter what its vista-depths, has never enjoyed and will never enjoy the almost reverential awe that is accorded to the written word. This is in one sense as it ought to be, for it is the written word that enshrines most permanently and gloriously the traditions we are so proud of. But it is also true that books, the most stable form of the written word, often enough are regarded with an almost religious deference. This can be seen in the esteem enjoyed by authors—almost any authors. To have written a book (!) elevates a man, in popular esteem, almost to the realms of the gods. Any number of people, perhaps the professional bookmen in particular, who would heartily approve an immediate and dry-eyed junking of the film version of *Forever Amber* (what a trashy film, they would aver) would rise in organized protest against any concerted action to have it banned as a book.

Still, there is some justice in this stand. A book is indeed a book, and the distribution of books, especially in this age of the cheaply priced paper-covered editions, poses problems that do not pester the films. Or perhaps better, the problems faced and to whatever degree solved by the Legion of Decency are not the precise problems faced by the NODL. Hence the consideration given above to the work of the Legion and the solutions suggested about the charges of pressure and boycott leveled against the Legion cannot be applied to the NODL *in toto*. We shall have to make some modifications, which will lead us immediately into the distinction again between *the* Catholic viewpoint on censorship and divergent viewpoints held by various Catholics.

What is the NODL? What are its purposes? How does it operate? What are the charges made against it, and what is the validity of the charges?

We shall start here, as we did in considering the Legion of Decency, by allowing the NODL to speak for itself. This sort of self-appraisal has, as a matter of fact, already been made in public more than once. The reader may consult, for example, the article, "NODL States Its Case," in the June 1, 1957, issue of *America*, a national Catholic weekly review. Therein Monsignor Thomas J. Fitzgerald, executive secretary of the National Office for Decent Literature, essayed, by calm analysis of the NODL's purposes and practices, to reply to the charges of the ACLU which have been referred to earlier in this volume. Of value, too, to one who would like to explore further the NODL's view of itself is an interview with Monsignor Fitzgerald which appeared in the May 20, 1957, *Publishers' Weekly*.

To go directly to the source, however, it seems good to reproduce here the exact information that is supplied to anyone who inquires about the NODL. The following documents are from the NODL headquarters in Chicago and will be furnished to any interested party. It will be noted that the documents provide not only a general statement of purposes but some practical "procedure sheets" as well. We shall comment on both these aspects of NODL's work later.

WHAT IS NODL?

The Catholic bishops of the United States established the National Office for Decent Literature in December of 1938. Its purpose, as stated by the Episcopal Committee, was "to set in motion the moral forces of the entire country . . . against the lascivious type of literature which threatens moral, social, and national life."

In no sense did the bishops consider NODL exclusively a Catholic movement. On the contrary, they appealed to *all* moral forces to combat the plague of indecent literature. NODL was, and is, merely a service organization which coordinates activities and supplies information to all interested groups, regardless of race, color, or creed.

In 1938 NODL was concerned only with magazines, and, from a national office in Fort Wayne, Indiana, published a list of those it found objectionable for youth. Since the appearance on the market of the modern comic book and pocket-size book, NODL has also been evaluating publications in these two fields.

In April 1955 NODL moved to 33 E. Congress Parkway, Chicago 5, Illinois. Its purpose remains the same as that set as its goal in 1938.

THE NODL CODE

The National Office for Decent Literature has been established to safeguard the moral and spiritual ideals of youth through a program designed:

1. To remove objectionable comic books, magazines, and pocket-size books from places of distribution accessible to youth;

2. to encourage the publication of good literature;

3. to promote plans to develop worthwhile reading habits during youth's formative years.

NODL fulfills its purpose, in part, by offering to responsible individuals and organizations evaluations of current comic books, magazines, and pocket-size books based on clearly defined, objective standards.

Publications are listed as objectionable for youth which:

1. Glorify crime or the criminal;

2. Describe in detail ways to commit criminal acts;

3. Hold lawful authority in disrespect;

4. Exploit horror, cruelty, or violence;

5. Portray sex facts offensively;

6. Feature indecent, lewd, or suggestive photographs or illustrations;

7. Carry advertising which is offensive in content or advertise products which may lead to physical or moral harm;

8. Use blasphemous, profane, or obscene speech indiscriminately and repeatedly;

9. Hold up to ridicule any national, religious, or racial group.

NODL VOLUNTEER REVIEWING COMMITTEES

Since the establishment of the Comics Code Authority, comic books are reviewed only once a year unless a request is made for evaluation of a particular title. Mothers of grammar-school or teen-age children compose this reviewing board.

The chairman of a group of five mothers receives a specified number of comic books. Each member of the group reads each book in the light of the NODL Code and evaluates it as (1) unobjectionable, (2) borderline, or (3) objectionable. If all five reviewers find the book unobjectionable, it is added to the NODL acceptable list. If four of the five mothers consider the book unsuitable, it is placed on the NODL objectionable list. If they vote it borderline, NODL takes no further action.

All magazines are reviewed once each year (single titles on request at any time) by specially qualified committees of men and women. One person reads the magazine, writes an opinion of it based on the Code, and returns it to NODL. Then five other reviewers examine the publication to determine the validity of the original reviewer's judgment. Thus, a magazine cannot be placed on the objectionable list until six persons have agreed that it violates the NODL Code.

Carefully selected, competent reviewers use the same method employed for magazines in evaluating pocket-size books. These reviewers must have a college background. Many members of the Protestant and Jewish faiths serve on this reviewing board.

PARISH DECENCY CRUSADE
(Instruction and Procedure Sheet)

I. Visit your pastor, tell him about the coming campaign, and ask his advice and help. Remember that you and your committee are directly responsible to him at all times.

II. Call a meeting of committee members. Go over the procedure instructions with them. Tell them that other religious and civic groups may shortly be starting similar campaigns. Emphasize that the interest of other groups should not lessen, but intensify their efforts.

PROCEDURE

I. Make a list of all places, including newsstands, in your parish that sell comic books, magazines, and pocket-size books.

II. Divide the committee into teams of two members each. Assign not more than three dealers to each team.

III. Explain that future success may depend on the impression the team makes on the first visit. Experience suggests the following steps.

A. The team visits the store at a slack time when the owner or manager is not too busy to talk to them.

B. A team member outlines the purpose of the Decency Crusade, if it is not already known, always stressing that its *sole aim is to protect the ideals and morality of our boys and girls.*

C. The team gives the dealer an NODL list, which he may keep, and asks permission to examine the racks, not only on that occasion, but at weekly intervals thereafter.

D. The team explains that future visits are made in a spirit of co-operation. Most dealers have not the time to check their racks regularly, and the team offers to do it for them.

E. If objectionable titles are on display, a team member courteously asks that they be removed from sale. If the dealer agrees, the team thanks him. If he refuses, the team leaves quietly, and reports the refusal to the pastor, who can determine future action.

IV. Order from NODL, 33 E. Congress Parkway, Chicago 5, Illinois, enough lists on a yearly subscription basis to supply each dealer with one each month. NODL lists may also be given to any responsible individual or organization.

V. *Caution:* NODL urges committee members to make sure lists do not fall into the hands of adolescents. It warns especially against posting them on bulletin boards or reprinting them in parish bulletins or neighborhood newspapers.

VI. NODL is ready to help the Decency Committee at any time.

CITIZENS' COMMITTEES

In many cities the campaign against objectionable literature is conducted on a community-wide basis under a citizens' committee, which may be organized and activated in the following manner:

I. An individual organization or a prominent citizen:

A. Invites the president of every civic, educational, social, fraternal, and religious organization interested in the welfare of youth to attend a preliminary meeting;

B. Appoints a general chairman.

II. The preliminary meeting, at which the general chairman presides, should include the following:

A. A display of samples of objectionable literature on sale locally that should be of civic concern;

B. A brief, but thorough and well-prepared, talk on the problem;

C. Organization of a citizens' committee composed of representatives of each organization in attendance;

D. Discussion to determine the purpose and function of the citizens' committee. In this connection, citing the experience of other communities is helpful. Citizens' groups customarily:

   1. Visit all retail outlets and request dealers to remove objectionable publications from sale;

   2. Promote plans for developing good reading habits in children;

   3. Sponsor necessary legislation to curb the evil of indiscriminate distribution of objectionable publications.

E. After thorough discussion, appointment by the general chairman of a temporary committee is made to *determine a plan of action*.

F. The date of another meeting to be held within one month is fixed.

G. Adjournment.

III. Well in advance of the second meeting:

A. The report of the temporary committee is sent to each interested organization;

B. Each organization is asked to vote immediately on affiliation with the Civic Decent Literature Committee;

C. Promptly after voting to affiliate, the organization appoints a Decent Literature Chairman to commit the organization to the plan of action outlined in the report of the temporary committee.

IV. At the second meeting:

A. The various Decent Literature chairmen affiliate their organizations;

B. The general chairman appoints a subcommittee to draw up a constitution and bylaws;

C. When the Civic Decent Literature Committee has acquired sufficient information on the type of material available to youth, the general chairman should appoint a subcommittee to meet with the local distributor to discuss the co-operation they may expect from him;

D. The general chairman should also appoint a group of lawyers to act as a legal advisory committee. These lawyers should make a thorough study of the present legal thinking on obscenity. After this research the legal committee should be able to advise on legal steps to take and legislation to sponsor, and also restrain the committee from overstepping legal bounds.

V. A sample constitution and the procedure used by other civic groups in visiting retail outlets may be obtained by writing the National Office for Decent Literature, 33 E. Congress Parkway, Chicago 5, Illinois.

SUGGESTED PROCEDURE FOR CITIZENS' COMMITTEES
(*Must be modified to meet local conditions*)

I. The General Chairman

A. Asks each organization participating to appoint a Decent Literature chairman and, at a meeting called for the purpose,

B. Explains the purpose of the crusade and the procedure;

C. Assigns a definite territory to each organization to prevent duplication of effort;

D. Instructs the Decent Literature chairmen to return to their own organizations, recruit committee members, and explain to committee members the purpose and procedure of the crusade.

II. The Decent Literature Chairman

A. Makes a list of all places, including newsstands, within his territory, that sell comic books, magazines and pocket-size books;

B. Divides his committee into two-man teams and assigns not more than three dealers to each team;

C. Briefs the team on how to make the first visit most effective:

   1. The team visits the store at a time when the owner or manager is not too busy to talk to them;

   2. A team member outlines the purpose of the Decency Crusade, if it is not already known, always stressing its

sole purpose, which is to protect the ideals and morality of our boys and girls;

3. After giving the dealer an NODL list, which he may keep, the team asks permission to examine the racks, not only on that occasion, but at weekly intervals thereafter;

4. Future visits, the team explains, are made in a spirit of co-operation. Because most dealers have not the time to check their racks regularly, the team offers to do it for them;

5. If the team finds no objectionable publications, it commends the owner or manager;

6. If the team finds objectionable titles, it courteously asks that they be removed from sale;

7. If the dealer refuses to co-operate, the team leaves quietly. Little is ever gained by argument, but silence can often be most effective;

8. Each team reports the results of its visits to its Decent Literature chairman, who in turn reports to the general chairman. In this way, the Citizens' Committee is kept aware of progress.

III. Use of NODL Lists

A. Committees using NODL lists should order enough on a yearly subscription basis to permit teams to leave a current list with each dealer each month. To subscribe to lists, write, National Office for Decent Literature, 33 E. Congress Parkway, Chicago 5, Illinois.

B. If a committee alters the NODL list—by adding or deleting titles—NODL's name may not be used in connection with the revised list.

C. *Caution*: NODL urges committee members to make sure lists do not fall into the hands of adolescents. It warns especially against posting them on bulletin boards or reprinting them in neighborhood newspapers.

GENERAL INFORMATION ON ORGANIZATION

(Compiled from a survey made among persons who have actually worked on Decent Literature campaigns)

Membership of Committees: The Decent Literature Committee may be composed of men or women, or both.

Preparing the Merchants: Before starting a drive, some organizations send a letter to the merchants, telling them about the campaign and explaining the methods used. Thus, the dealers are prepared for the first visit from committee members.

Identification: Many organizations give workers identification cards to make their introduction to merchants more official.

Use of Lists: A list of objectionable publications is necessary to indicate to the dealer the books and magazines which should be removed from sale. Some local groups compile their own lists, based on a Code of Decency determined by their own membership.

The NODL List: For organizations that do not find it convenient to prepare their own lists, NODL provides a monthly list of current objectionable magazines and pocket-size books and acceptable comic books that have been evaluated according to the NODL Code.

Permission to Use the NODL List: Any responsible group which of its own volition and choosing decides to use the NODL list in its campaign has NODL's permission to do so. NODL indicates, however, that the list is merely an expression of a publication's nonconformity with the NODL Code, and states categorically that the list is not to be used for purposes of legal action, boycott, or coercion.

How to Obtain NODL Lists: NODL lists of publications found objectionable for youth may be obtained from the National Office for Decent Literature at an individual subscription price of 75 cents a year. Prices on quantity lots on request.

QUESTIONS THE DEALER MAY ASK

(Questions that storekeepers ask committee members fall into a pattern. Here are a few of the more common queries, with suggested answers.)

Q.: Why pick on me? The distributor makes me take a lot of this junk in order to get the good stuff.

A.: The dealer may have a legitimate case. However, this complaint has not the justification it once had, because the block buying or job-lot policy is now illegal in most states because of the enactment of "tie-in sale" laws. If a dealer insists that he is forced to take the bad in order to get the good, obtain his name and the name and address of his distributor. Write to the distributor, or contact him personally, to ascertain if such is the case.

Q.: Why don't you go to the publisher?

A.: It is true that now and then a reputable publisher lets an objectionable work get into print. NODL knows these publishers and can work with them. However, most of the objectionable publications are put out deliberately by operators who know that they will sell, and who care nothing about their harmful effect on youth. They cannot be reasoned with.

Q.: Why are only Catholics interested in these publications?

A.: It is not true that only Catholics are interested. On the contrary, in all parts of the country groups composed of religious, civic, and fraternal organizations are constantly increasing in number and activity as public opinion is becoming more aware of the danger of these publications to youth.

Q.: What is NODL doing to encourage good reading habits among young people?

A.: NODL accepts its responsibility to promote good reading for youth. It already has a list of acceptable comic books and recently published the third of its partial list of acceptable pocket-size books for young people. NODL will strive to keep its lists of acceptable reading current. As other methods of fostering acceptable literature for youth are investigated, the results will be made available.

ON THE POSITIVE SIDE

An appreciation of good literature, fostered from early childhood, helps to shape mind and character into good citizenship. The program suggested below highlights various methods to achieve this result:

1. Parents should know the type of literature their child reads, both inside and outside the home. They should try to develop in the child a love of good literature, coupled with an enthusiasm to read.

2. Parents should set a good example by reading good books themselves and discussing them in the family circle.

3. Parents should know the books listed on their child's required reading program at school and make sure the child reads them intelligently. If the school library is inadequate because of a limited budget, the PTA should volunteer to correct the situation.

4. Parents should encourage the child to take every advantage of the local public library.

5. Parents should urge the child to buy books with money from his weekly allowance. With so many worthwhile books in paperback today, he can accumulate an excellent library at little cost.

6. To make inexpensive reprints easily accessible, a paperback bookstore in the school may be manned by the students

themselves, with the profits set aside for school activities.

7. Both parents and community groups should compliment publishers, wholesalers, and retailers who stock good literature.

8. Community groups should help the local libraries by promotional campaigns and financial aid.

9. Community groups should sponsor book fairs, book reviews, and private libraries to interest their members in good reading, so that these members may in turn interest their children.

Criticism of the NODL by anti-censorship forces has been steady and vocal since the very beginning of the NODL's career. Its basic purpose—namely, "to set in motion the moral forces of the entire country . . . against the lascivious type of literature which threatens moral, social and national life" —and in particular as such literature is readily available to youth, is, or ought to be, a purpose with which all would agree —certainly *the* Catholic viewpoint on censorship would back up such a purpose. But such a purpose obviously connotes action, and it is as soon as we move into the field of even the most initial action that the conflict arises.

Criticism of the NODL rose to a new intensity in the year 1956–57. This new impulse was largely given by an article that appeared in the October 1956 issue of *Harper's* magazine. Authored by editor John Fischer, it was entitled "The Harm That Good Men Do," and sparked a veritable forest fire of condemnatory comments on the NODL. Mr. Fischer's attack was answered in the pages of *America* by Reverend John Courtney Murray, S.J. (November 3, 1956), in an article titled "The Bad Arguments Intelligent Men Make." Though Father Murray neatly spiked some of Mr. Fischer's allegations, he had some criticism to level against the NODL, to which we shall advert farther on. By way of parenthesis here, it is good to applaud the American Book Publishers Council for a nice gesture of fair play. The Council had distributed offprints of Mr. Fischer's article, and when Father Murray's rejoinder was called to its attention the Council sent reprints of it to the same audience who had received the attack. In like manner, the ACLU distributed offprints of Monsignor Fitzgerald's "The NODL States Its Case." These documents are given in full in the Appendices.

But what is puzzling, in view of these honest efforts at having the problem seen in full by both sides of the controversy, is the fact that misrepresentations of the NODL still get repeated and have been repeated so often that most people are probably now convinced that they are true. So, for instance, the ACLU continues to claim that the NODL recommends or even actually employs the use of "good-conduct" seals. Says the ACLU's "Statement" to which we have referred: "Newsdealers, druggists and others who agree in advance not to sell anything to which the NODL objects are given monthly certificates of compliance." But Monsignor Fitzgerald, in his *Publishers' Weekly* interview (p. 15), has stated that "the NODL office *discourages the use of seals of compliance* only from a practical viewpoint—a merchant may stop cooperating after a few months and still will have his seal." It may be that many would have liked to hear Monsignor Fitzgerald say that the NODL discourages the use of such seals or certificates *on principle*, but the simple fact remains that wherever a local group, acting under the inspiration of the NODL, actually does make use of such seals it is not paying attention to the "discouragement" of the National Office. But one would never gather this fact from the statements of the ACLU.

Again, in a letter of July 6, 1957, lawyer Morris L. Ernst, then vice-chairman of the ACLU, wrote to enlist support for the "Statement."[1] He claimed that "this extremest group [the NODL] is actively campaigning to have books of which *it* does not approve banned from libraries and bookstores." But the NODL has stated time and again that the literature that stirs its concern is merely the comic book, the paper-backed book, and the magazines that are available to youth at a nominal price and that it is not concerned with the field of adult reading. Libraries and bookstores (as distinguished from newsstands and drugstores) simply fall outside the scope of its activities.

The crucial point of criticism, however, is the use that is made by law-enforcement bodies or individuals of the NODL's lists of "Publications Disapproved for Youth." The classic case cropped up in Youngstown, Ohio, in 1953. Armed

[1] Refer to Appendices.

with an NODL list, the chief of police ordered newsdealers to clear their stands of disapproved material, threatening penalties upon failure to comply. The case went to the courts and the decision was that the officer had exceeded his authority; the books could be banned from distribution only after they might be found to violate the state obscenity laws. Such action has been duplicated time and again all over the country, and frequently the use of an NODL list has entered into the action.

How does the NODL view such use of its lists?

"The NODL office denies that it has ever recommended or encouraged any arbitrary coercive police action. Such is not the purpose or procedure of the NODL. Under existing laws in most communities, duly constituted police officers have the obligation of taking action against vendors of obscene publications. In the initial action the police power must be employed only to arrest the vendor and must be limited to a specific publication (or publications) considered obscene under the law. The final decision as to whether the law has in fact been violated lies with the courts. . . ."[2]

It must be said in all frankness that it is slightly difficult more often than not to determine precisely what the ACLU objects to in a particular instance. Thus the charge is made and repeated that the NODL resorts to "boycott"; but the ACLU's own policy statement recognized, "as far as legal right is concerned, the use of such orderly and lawful means as peaceful and unobstructive picketing and the organization of a specific and primary boycott even when they imply some degree of coercion." Then, however, the same policy statement goes on to deplore, "in the field of communication," any form of "general or secondary boycott—designed, for example, to close a theatre entirely [may we legitimately substitute here "bookseller, newsdealer"?] or to close other theatres whose proprietors ally themselves with the proprietor of the first theatre." This sort of boycott, it is charged, is "especially contrary to the spirit of the Constitution" in the field of communication. But it has never been the goal of the NODL— nor of any of the autonomous groups who act under NODL

[2] Monsignor Fitzgerald in *America*, June 1, 1957, p. 282.

inspiration—to close down newsdealers, drugstores, or other channels through which the "objectionable" material is marketed. As in the case of the Legion of Decency, the boycott result of the NODL is secondary. Indeed, in the "procedure sheets" quoted above, one will search in vain for a mention of the word; the committee who waits on the dealer is to "leave silently" if the dealer refuses to remove the material. The fact that the committee returns every two weeks to renew its request is interpreted by the ACLU as "encouraging" the creation of a "public-morals police-force." This is surely indictment by epithet.

It is not a very happy nor indeed a very fruitful task to have to point out what seem to be deliberate misrepresentations of the purposes and procedures of the NODL, for such a procedure gives this book a controversial tone that is not its intent. But if we are to discuss the NODL in our attempt to assess *the* Catholic viewpoint on censorship, or the viewpoint of Catholics, it is imperative that we judge the NODL for what it actually is and is actually trying to do, not for what a distorted picture of it may be. As a good example of how the distorted picture grows in the public mind, consider the following. Shortly after the ACLU issued its appeal for authors, publishers, editors, and the like to sign their "Statement" of May 1957, the magazine *America* editorialized on the indictment of the NODL, to which some 168 people had affixed their signatures.[3] Among other points raised, the editorial asked of the ACLU this question: "We wonder . . . if the distinguished authors who stood behind ACLU's exaggerated charges have ever read the policy statements of the NODL. Did ACLU send to each of them a copy of the NODL's charter? Does each one of them know accurately just what the NODL is and is trying to do?" To this, Patrick Murphy Malin, executive director of the ACLU, replied in a letter to *America's* editor (August 14): "No, but the description of the NODL's purposes and code in our statement is an accurate summary; and the signers (who, if they had asked, could have obtained a copy of the NODL's charter from us) are well-informed people."

[3] *America*, May 18, 1957, p. 218.

Now, if the charge is made that the NODL, for all its good intentions and noble purposes, is still not aware of responsibilities which it has willy-nilly incurred and cannot shrug off (such a charge was made in an editorial in the same issue of *Publishers' Weekly* that carried Monsignor Fitzgerald's interview), cannot the same be said of the ACLU? First, as we have indicated, it is by no means sure that the ACLU's summary *is* "accurate." Second, it is doubtful that the 168 signers of the "Statement," well informed as they may be on many things, were completely familiar with the purposes and procedures of the NODL. It is to be very much doubted that Eleanor Roosevelt, for instance, who was one of the signers, ever had the chance to do more to inform herself about the NODL than to read the ACLU's summary. There is every reasonable ground for suspecting that most of the 168 signers signed for the sole reason that since they were informed that the NODL's activities are against the spirit of the Constitution they felt that their Americanism would be suspect if they did not sign. (It may be of interest, though it proves nothing one way or the other, that, according to a list supplied by the NODL to the present writer, 267 authors, editors, etc., approached by the ACLU to sign the "Statement" did *not* lend their signatures; many of them clearly would have signed if they had "got around to it.")

So much for the regrettable recounting of charges and countercharges. As must be clear by now, in the present atmosphere the whole controversy boils down to this: the anti-censorship phalanx, headed by the ACLU, asserts that the NODL violates the spirit, if not the letter, of traditional American freedom of the press, as guaranteed by the First and Fourteenth Amendments, and the NODL flatly denies any such allegation. At any rate, this much seems to be clear. First, the NODL obviously engages in no *prior* censorship; it seeks to control the distribution of books (with reference only to the young) *after* they have got into the market place. The NODL does apply subsequent (repressive) censorship, primarily by an aroused public opinion, to which it will supply practical procedures if they are sought, and secondarily through the implication of possible boycott. These means may be called "extra-legal," but it is a far cry from "extra-legal" to "in violation of the spirit of the Constitution."[4]

In practical terms, the objections of the ACLU, the Book Publishers Council, and other groups who contest the democratic character of such an organization as the NODL boil down to this very definite situation. If the NODL, even granted that it acts within the letter of the law, succeeds in persuading a newsstand operator to remove some reading matter to which it objects, it is thereby depriving some, perhaps a majority, of American citizens in that locality of free access to reading matter which they do not agree is objectionable. Their "right to read" is curtailed because a minority group has imposed its moral judgment on a situation in which the American citizen is legally free. The NODL agrees that any citizen is legally free to read anything that has not been declared by law a violation of obscenity statutes; but it maintains that a good citizen, if alerted by morally aroused public opinion, will be willing to waive this legal right for the common good, especially as it touches the young. This may, indeed, be an idealistic hope on the part of the NODL, and perhaps it is asking too much; we shall return to this point later on.

Actually, the entire debate would seem to hinge on the question of the *availability* of reading matter the NODL considers unfit for the young. I believe that, as long as pornographic literature is being produced, just so long such literature ought to be available *somewhere* for *some persons*. That may seem shocking, but let me explain. Certainly a sociologist

[4] In a letter to the author in January 1961, Monsignor Thomas Fitzgerald, Executive Secretary of the NODL, writes as follows: "At the time your book was written [1957] the ACLU was fanning the flames of controversy. However, Patrick Murphy Malin [Executive Director of the ACLU] and I had already at that time begun a correspondence, which lasted over the period of a year. Since that time, ACLU has issued no public statements against NODL nor has it used the funds it collected to wage a campaign against it. This is not to say that we have reached a complete accord, but rather that ACLU has a better understanding of the aims and purposes of NODL. In this connection, I think the Bishops' statement on censorship [see Appendix E] did a great deal to dispel confusion." This development is one realization of the hopes expressed in the chapter to follow, on " 'Pressure Groups,' Boycott, and Co-operation."

or a historian or someone else with professional interest ought to be able to study this element in the "cultural" history of a nation. Roman Martial's epigrams, for instance (and they are about as foul as can be imagined), are certainly not for the pastime reading of the young and impressionable, but they are invaluable tools for the study of one element in the decline and fall of Roman civilization. Our current suggestive "art" and "girlie" magazines ought to be available for those who have reason to examine them—say, in public libraries where they could be restricted to properly concerned adults.

But does a private citizen have a legal *right* to be able to find *any* reading matter just short of the legally obscene *anywhere* any reading matter is sold? Suppose an individual newsstand proprietor decided entirely on his own that he would simply not stock "art"-photography magazines. Could his clientele charge that he was depriving them of a "right" to find such stuff on his stand? Suppose this proprietor made up his own list of material he would not sell? Would he not be imposing his own individual judgment on the supposed wishes and "rights" of those who patronize his stand? Yet the American Book Publishers Council, in its "Censorship Bulletin," counsels just such individual action:[5]

"The crux of the matter is the use of a list, any list, as a means of pressure or suasion upon sellers as opposed to readers. . . . It is wrong in principle, since sellers of publications should exercise, rather than abdicate to any group or list, their own moral responsibilities. Such use is also wrong in principle, because, to the degree to which it is successful, the consequence is that by the private judgment of a single group all others are denied the chance to buy and read what they please, wholly lawful though the publications may be. . . .

"Would it not be better . . . for the NODL groups' work with sellers to be confined to encouraging them to exercise their own independent moral judgment with respect to the general type of publications they offer for sale? . . ."

This, to say the least, is as "idealistic" a suggestion as the NODL's that adults willingly forfeit their legal right to expect to get whatever they want to read anywhere and every-

[5] December 1956, Vol. 1, No. 6.

where. It supposes, quite unrealistically, that proprietors of newsstands, etc., are familiar with the contents of every magazine, comic book, paper-backed book they sell. Second, it seems even more "undemocratic" and "un-American" than the activities of the NODL groups, for it places the decision on who shall read what squarely in the hands of one man, the proprietor, whereas the NODL's decision as to whether such-and-such material is objectionable is at least made in the give-and-take of group discussion before anyone starts trying to persuade the proprietor. How a one-man list is preferable to a committee-drawn list escapes me—unless, of course, the lurking fear is that a committee-drawn list (an NODL committee, obviously) is bound to reflect Catholic standards. But might not a one-man list, depending on the man, reflect Catholic or Jewish or atheistic or Communist or what-have-you points of view?

The arguments pro and con the NODL must by now seem to the reader to have got exactly nowhere. This, I am afraid, is true, and we may profitably hark back to the sage observation of Zechariah Chafee, Jr.:

"It is useless to define free speech [and freedom to read] by talk about rights . . . Each side takes the position of the man who was arrested for swinging his arms and hitting another in the nose, and asked the judge if he did not have a right to swing his arms in a free country. 'Your right to swing your arms ends just where the other man's nose begins.' To find the boundary line of any right, we must get behind rules of law to human facts . . . It must never be forgotten that the balancing cannot properly be done unless all the interests involved are adequately ascertained, and the great evil of all this talk about rights is that each side is so busy denying the other's claims to rights that it entirely overlooks the human desires and needs behind that claim."[6]

A feature writer in the Chicago *Daily News* ("Jack Mabley's Story," May 7, 1957) gives a dramatic account of what happens when debate of respective "rights" ignores "human wants and desires." While the "running battle," as he calls it, between the NODL and the ACLU continues, "your children

[6] *Op. cit.*, pp. 31–32.

are able to walk the streets to the nearest newsstand and revel in the worst printed filth this city has seen in generations." This columnist's conclusions sum up well the hope in which this book was written: "Somewhere between the alleged extremes of the NODL methods and the zeal of ACLU to guard civil rights should exist an area of intelligent moderation where both groups could agree on an effective means of combating obscenity."

But if the NODL's "rights" have not here been completely vindicated against the "rights" of those whom the ACLU and others are seeking to protect from invasion, at least the reader may have come to the conclusion that the picture is not quite so simple as either a member of the ACLU or a zealous and militant Catholic NODLer may have thought it to be. Further, a judgment not merely on the legal validity of the NODL's work but, even more, a judgment on the prudence and public-relations aspect of its activities is not as clear cut as a similar judgment on the purposes and practices of the Legion of Decency. This is true not only because the Legion is more experienced as an effective organization (it has learned much over the years, as well as teaching much) but also, as I have indicated earlier, because of the nature of the medium the NODL seeks to some extent to control. In addition, since the very nature of the NODL's practical group activities focuses on hundreds of neighborhood situations, it comes more immediately to the public eye. It must seem to the ACLU, as it scans censorship activity in our land, that the NODL is, so to speak, under every bed. The Legion's activities rarely work down to an immediate community level (individual instances of picketing are not, however, unknown, although they form no part of the recommendations of the National Office); but the NODL's practical work, if it is to have any effect, has to reach the local newsstand in your neighborhood. Inevitably, granted the purpose of the NODL, this leads to the impression that the NODL is much more of a "pressure group" than the Legion (whether pressure groups are good or bad will be taken up in the next chapter).

This observation, for what it is worth, leads us directly to the fact of varying Catholic opinions on the NODL. There is not, as much as it may surprise some, a monolithic Catholic consensus on the detailed activities of the NODL. There *is*, we hope, unanimous Catholic consensus on the desirability of keeping salacious, in addition to obviously obscene, reading matter out of the hands of the young; but not all Catholics who have tried to think the matter through will agree on all the details of the NODL's work. Here we are on ground where we must tread carefully, for the NODL is a creation of the corporate American hierarchy and, as such, demands and deserves the fealty of all American Catholics. But fealty to the purposes does not automatically forestall all and any raising of questions that touch on a matter of prudential operation in particular circumstances.

We must start, I take it, with four principles that have been best expressed by Reverend John Courtney Murray, S.J., in his reply to the *Harper* article by John Fischer. Father Murray, it will be remembered, was answering Mr. Fischer, not merely to refute some of his charges against the NODL, but, more importantly, in the conviction that "the foundations of our democracy are indeed laid in an identifiable consensus. But they are more importantly laid in a reasonable disposition to argue our many disagreements in intelligent and temperate fashion, using restrained language, avoiding misstatements, overstatements or simplifications, and endeavoring to define issues with precision in the light of all the relevant principles and facts."[7]

Toward this most laudable end, Father Murray posits the "practical rules that should govern the action of minority groups in a pluralistic society, in their legitimate effort to improve public morality." These rules are:

[7] *America*, "The Bad Arguments Intelligent Men Make," November 3, 1956, p. 120. This may be the apposite place to deplore the use that has consistently been made of Father Murray's position as declared in this article. In the ACLU "Statement" and in many other references to the censorship debate, Father Murray is consistently held up as a God-sent "liberal" who abhors the "extremist" NODL. This is simply not true. Father Murray's article expresses doubts about *some* of the NODL's practices; it does not repudiate either the NODL's purposes nor *all* of its practical steps. Father Murray needs no defense from the present writer, but the use to which his few differences with the NODL have been put is a flagrant example of the "bad arguments intelligent men make."

"First, within the larger pluralist society each minority group has the right to censor *for its own members*, if it so chooses, the content of the various media of communication, with a view to punishing the communication of materials that are judged to be harmful according to the special standards held within one group.

"Second, in a pluralist society no minority group has the right to demand that government should impose a general censorship, *affecting all the citizenry*, upon any medium of communication, with a view to punishing the communication of materials that are judged to be harmful to the special standards held within one group.

"Third, any minority group has the right to work toward the elevation of standards of public morality in the pluralist society, through the methods of *persuasion and pacific argument*.

"Fourth, in a pluralist society a group has no right to impose its own religious or moral views on other groups, *through the use of the methods of force, coercion, or violence*." (Emphases added.)[8]

The nub of the violent objections to the NODL by anti-censorship groups and of the uneasy questions that some Catholics pose to themselves regarding the NODL's operations lies in the third and fourth principles. The NODL will maintain that it works, not only in its central office, but in the individual groups across the country, in accordance with the third principle: namely, it is striving to "elevate the standards of public morality through the methods of persuasion and pacific argument." The ACLU and other bodies, however, charge that the NODL actually operates in the fashion cautioned against in the fourth principle: it tries to "im-

---

[8] *The Catholic Mind*, December 1956, p. 666. These rules appear in an article, "Literature and Censorship" (pp. 665–76), which was originally an address before the Thomas More Association, Chicago, and appeared first in *Books on Trial* (June–July 1956). In his *America* article, Father Murray acknowledges his indebtedness for the four principles to Professor Vernon J. Bourke of St. Louis University. Professor Bourke's paper in which they were posited will be found in full in *Problems of Communication in a Pluralistic Society* (Marquette University Press, 1956).

pose" its minority moral views through force and coercion, though certainly not through violence.

It is undeniable that there is some form of coercion implicit in the practical operations of the NODL. It is a moral coercion, a social pressure that is brought to bear on the newsstand operator, for instance. If it is simply *that* kind of coercion, neither Father Murray nor any other Catholic pondering the problem of censorship would have objections, for coercion of that type is actually distinguished with difficulty from "persuasion." But unfortunately the coercion that is connected in the popular mind with the NODL has, from time to time and spottily over the country, been much more frightening and severe. I refer again to the use made by police-enforcement agencies of the NODL list of "disapproved" material. When a police officer strides into Joe Brown's corner store and orders Joe to get rid of some "literature" and brandishes an NODL list in his face, Joe understandably wonders whether the minion of the law was not *sent* on his mission by the NODL's national office in Chicago; how is he to know otherwise? More, if Joe entertains ideas about the Catholic Church that so many do, to the effect that it is bent on imposing Catholic moral standards on the unsuspecting public, he will probably think that "the Church" is out to wreck his business. The local representative of the ACLU gets wind of the supposed coercion, the publisher of some of the "disapproved" material is alerted, and we have a case for the courts, something that the NODL never intended and actually has no interest in.

But the NODL must have an interest, as Father Murray and others have pointed out, in the public-relations aspects of the use to which its lists are put. This is the crucial point of some Catholic questioning of the NODL's methods and, if I may interject what I am convinced is the answer, it lies precisely in the fact that the NODL is not as tightly organized as it is commonly thought to be. On a few occasions the national office in Chicago has publicly protested the use to which its lists have been put by police-enforcing agencies, but the same office will tell an inquirer that it is simply not able to keep track of such misuses of the list whenever they spring up over the country. One of the great strengths of the ACLU, for instance, is its alertness to detect and publicize any actions it considers infringements of civil rights; in this it does a most efficient job, and our controversy with the organization in this matter of censorship is not to be construed as a lack of sympathy with the great good the ACLU does in the general field of such rights. But unfortunately the ACLU betrays that it does not realize how loosely at times some Catholic national agencies are organized. Some of these organizations are given credit for being much more tight-knit than they are or want to be.

Some Catholic students of the censorship problem, however, feel that the NODL cannot have it two ways. If it is to distribute its lists of disapproved books far and wide, it must also assume an equally far and wide supervision of the use of the lists.[9] It cannot logically assert that its lists are not to be used for the purpose of coercion and yet be indifferent to coercion (especially the most dictatorial kind) when it raises its head. The only answer to this, it would seem, is for the NODL to be *better* organized, and it is easy to imagine what shudders such a suggestion will occasion in some quarters.

Again, in some Catholic thought on the matter, the suspicion arises that perhaps the NODL is actually trying to do too much—that its net is spread too wide. There is the matter, for instance, of some of the pocket-size books, not a few of which have been written by Pulitzer and other prize-winning authors. It is probably true that such books come but rarely to the attention of adolescents. The possible harm done by such books has to be weighed against the probable and perhaps legitimate ill will caused by a suggestion that such books be withdrawn from general easy availability. The desirability of not listing

[9] In the January, 1961 letter of Monsignor Fitzgerald referred to above occurs the following reflection on this statement: "Actually, we now have 'watch dogs.' Through an agreement with the ACLU and the American Book Publishers' Council, in any instance where they can present evidence that the NODL listing is being misused, we will immediately write the offender and state our position. In the past two years, I believe there have been four instances where such action was necessary. In two of these instances, we had discovered the violation before it was reported, and had taken action on our own initiative."

such books as disapproved has recently become all the stronger because of the decision of the United States Supreme Court affecting the Michigan law. In a unanimous ruling on February 25, 1957, the Court reversed the conviction of a Michigan bookseller for violating the state obscenity statute by selling a paperbound reprint of *The Devil Rides Outside*, by John Griffin. Justice Felix Frankfurter, writing the opinion, declared:

"It is clear on the record that appellant was convicted because Michigan made it an offense for him to make available for the general reading public . . . a book that the trial judge found to have a potentially deleterious influence on youth. The State insists that, by thus quarantining the general reading public against books that are not too rugged for grown men and women in order to shield juvenile innocence, it is exercising its power to promote the general welfare. Surely, this is to burn the house to roast the pig. The effect of such a law would be to reduce the adult population of Michigan to reading only what is fit for children."[10]

It may be noted that this Court decision did not in this case touch on a definition of obscenity (that was to come later, in the June 24 decision), nor did it rule on the question whether a state could censor books on the basis of obscenity. Further, as Justice Frankfurter pointed out, the Court ruling did not leave the young people of Michigan without protection, for there exist in the state ample statutes covering the sale of obscene matter to youth. The NODL would and does admit that some books like *The Devil Rides Outside* can be read without harm by many adults, but it hopes that an aroused public opinion will lead the adults to waive their legal privilege of finding such books easily available.

This is certainly an idealistic stand, as we have mentioned, and the NODL would very likely be on firmer ground, and ground that would more easily win public support, if it restricted its disapproved lists to those magazines and comics that have no other discernible reason for existence than to arouse lewd, erotic, if not absolutely obscene interest. If it is

[10] *Butler* v. *Michigan*, quoted in the American Book Publishers Council "Censorship Bulletin," Vol. 1, No. 6 (December 1956).

rejoined that this would be to lower its standards, the response might be that not even the NODL can achieve everything in the way of cleaning up the channels where objectionable material is readily and cheaply available. Not even Canon Law, as we have tried to develop in Chapter III, attempts to control for Catholics literature that is vulgar, crude, suggestive; it restricts its extent to coping with the *ex professo* obscene. It is also quite true that neither the Legion nor the NODL is obliged to keep to the minimum envisioned by Canon Law; they may legitimately attempt more in an effort to elevate public taste and morals. Canon Law is concerned with a moral *minimum*; they are inculcating a spiritual ideal. But it still remains true that the spirit of Canon Law is the safe guide, and the very modesty of its legislation in this matter of censorship is probably the best assurance that obedience will be willingly given by those to whom the legislation is directed. If the NODL strove for less, it might achieve more. Further, without ceasing to work for a healthier-minded United States, it might reduce the points of friction with those who rebel at any form of "censorship."[11]

A third problem faced by the NODL again springs both from lack of a tightly knit organization and from the "grass-roots" level on which local committees operate. The reviewing staff at headquarters (whose operations are described above) is quite probably as qualified to pass moral judgment on lit-

[11] Since the original edition of *Catholic Viewpoint on Censorship*, the problem has taken on greater proportions in the field of paperbacks—as distinguished from magazines and comics. At least seventeen publishers of most questionable paperbacks have appeared on the scene, to such an extent that the NODL states that "this type of book has so swamped our office and taken up so much space on our NODL list that we have had little time to consider the work of the more reputable publishers."

When I phrased the original suggestion to the effect that the NODL might well consider restricting its operations to "magazines and comics," I had no intention of removing from its vigilance the sleazier type of paperback. What I had in mind was precisely the general output of the "more reputable publishers"; their productions might well be left unconsidered by the NODL. The point was that since not *all* distasteful, suggestive works can possibly be effectively protested against, the more efficient protest should be reserved for the greater evil.

erature as are the reviewers for the Legion of Decency, but the actual putting of that judgment into operation, through the distribution and "enforcement" of the lists, works out in ramifications that are much less controllable than those of the local activities of the Legion.

This leads to the distinct possibility of greater irresponsibility in local NODL operations. The overzealous are easily attracted, as Father Murray points out in his *America* article, to get something done in a hurry; whereas a critic acts most fruitfully precise when he is not motivated by "moral indignation." And moral indignation is indeed very easily aroused in any decent person when he passes almost any newsstand and glances at the foul "art" and "girlie" magazines displayed to catch those who are young, whether in years or impressionableness. But here again the spirit, and the actual letter, of Canon Law must be the norm; and not only the original reviewers of the magazines and books must be well versed in their subject but, as far as possible, the local committees working for their removal. They must know and be able to explain fairly and convincingly the difference between vulgarity and obscenity, between the positively dangerous and the regrettably coarse and vulgar. Then the danger will be lessened that the vendor will feel that he is being "ordered" to stop displaying what the NODL committee objects to; he may come more easily to see the reasoning and accept the suggestion, for, after all, he himself is very probably a good family man too. The NODL claims that it is exactly when a program is presented to a vendor on a basis of neighborliness (everybody knows the proprietor and his children and he knows his customers and their young ones) that the reasonableness of the NODL's crusade makes greatest headway. This subject of social improvement through local "extra-legal" activity will occupy our space in the concluding chapter.

These points of criticism of the NODL which have engaged the concern of some Catholics interested in the problems of censorship can be summed up by simply saying, it seems to me, that the big task facing the NODL is one of bettering its public-relations program. The American Book Publishers Council, the Authors League, and the ACLU will probably never heartily agree with the principles of the

NODL, for the basic reason that they do not agree with the concepts of law and freedom outlined in the first part of this book. But they may come to see—it is a hope worth fostering —that the practices of the NODL are not so objectionable as they now seem to them. At the very least, those practices may come to be more fairly represented to the general public, and the NODL's efforts to correct abuses when and where they occur may come to be given the applause they fully deserve. But it is without doubt in the spirit of the Church's legislation on censorship that the NODL must make those efforts in season and out.

CHAPTER IV

"Pressure Groups," Boycott, and Co-operation

In issuing its "Statement on Censorship Activity by Private Organizations and the National Organization for Decent Literature" (the NODL is now titled the National *Office* for Decent Literature), in May 1957, the American Civil Liberties Union stated: "In discussing this kind of censorship we make a clear distinction between the right of all organizations to express their opinion, which we defend, and acting in such a manner as to deny those who do not agree with their opinion an opportunity to read the literature themselves." In this connection the ACLU refers to its declaration of 1951, which it may be good to quote here in full. It is referred to as an "official policy statement" on "pressure-group censorship."

"The ACLU defends, as being within both the letter and the spirit of the Constitution, any simple expression by any individual or group of disapproval of the contents of any book, etc., or an attempt simply to dissuade others from buying it. It recognizes as far as legal right is concerned, the use of such orderly and lawful means as peaceful and unobstructive picketing and the organization of a specific and primary boycott even when they imply some degree of coercion. However, in view of the fact that the field of communication differs significantly from the general field of industry and commerce, the

Union actively opposes, as being especially contrary to the spirit of the Constitution, the use of such means in the following ways: (1) as pressure, or explicit threat thereof, at any time prior to the actual offering of a motion picture, etc. to the public; and (2) even after the actual offering to the public, in the form of a general or secondary boycott—designed, for example, to close a theatre entirely or to close other theatres whose proprietors ally themselves with the proprietor of the first theatre."

Though we shall return to the idea of the boycott later, it may be good to supply here the distinction between a primary and secondary boycott. A primary boycott occurs when a threat not to patronize is directed only against the offending party (employer, bookseller, film exhibitor, etc.); a secondary boycott arises when the threat not to patronize is extended to induce a third party or parties to join in the refusal of patronage.[1]

It is worth pointing out, too, that "boycott" is used in somewhat an analogous fashion when applied to cultural matters; its original meaning and its strict relevance is in matters of industrial, and especially labor, disputes. Its use in other fields has been sanctioned by custom; but it is always good to keep in mind that the application of the word in matters of, say, books and motion pictures has always to be carefully scrutinized.

As will be readily recognized, this statement of the ACLU includes, in so far as it bases a protest against both the Legion of Decency and the NODL, three indictments. Both organizations are accused of (1) exercising censorship, (2) being "pressure groups," and (3) exercising at least secondary boycotts. It is to be hoped that we have discussed sufficiently the matter of whether and to what extent the Legion and the NODL are actually censoring bodies. It shall now be the task to examine whether or not they are "pressure groups" and whether they employ and/or excite to boycott.

"Pressure group" is, in our day and age, getting to be more and more of a fighting word, though the fact of the existence

[1] Harry L. Laidler in the *Encyclopedia of the Social Sciences* (New York: Macmillan, 1931), Vol. II, p. 665, s.v. "Boycott."

of pressure groups is by no means always and inevitably a fighting fact. Pressure groups have existed in our history, both gloriously (the Boston Tea Party) and ingloriously (the minority that put across the Volstead Act); they now exist gloriously (the National Association for the Advancement of Colored People) and ingloriously (the "White Councils" blocking racial integration); they will continue to exist, more gloriously, let us hope, than otherwise. They are part and parcel of our democratic processes, and to use the appellation merely with a sneer, as is too frequently done, is to belittle the historical fact that such groups "in general have arisen because they satisfy some social need . . . they perform useful as well as objectionable functions . . . they are an integral as well as an indispensable part of the community. . . . Care must be taken to keep the over-all pressure-group picture in perspective. Shortcomings must not overshadow and obliterate the good."[2]

The same authority then goes on to enumerate some of the advantages that accrue to a democratic society by the presence and operation of "pressure groups."

"Their role is to help the public generally and government officials particularly to formulate public policy. . . . The principal reason for granting groups of people the right of association and freedom to express their opinions is the conviction that such freedom to advocate ideas, such competition for public support and governmental approval, are best calculated to insure an enlightened public opinion and wise public policy. . . . Pressure groups make their greatest contribution to the democratic process by taking an active part in the great competitive arena of ideas, expressions of opinion, and, if you wish, propaganda."[3]

The point of this kind of introduction to some observations on pressure groups is simply to indicate that the mere phrase gets us exactly nowhere. The essential problem is not whether

[2] Harwood L. Childs, professor of politics at Princeton University, on "Pressure Groups and Intellectual Freedom," in *Freedom of Communication*, proceedings of the First Conference on Intellectual Freedom, New York City, June 28–29, 1952 (Chicago: American Library Association, 1954), pp. 73–87.

[3] *Ibid.*

the Legion and the NODL can be *called* pressure groups but whether the pressure they bring to bear (if they actually do) is unconstitutional or at least contrary to the spirit of the Constitution and, consequently, undemocratic, un-American. It would be shouting against a hurricane to advocate the mutual banning of the charge, "You are just an old pressure group," but it would, I firmly believe, be one of the first steps toward getting on with an attempt at a co-operation which is the only solution to the problem and which I shall try to outline very tentatively in the concluding portion of this chapter.

So much for the preliminaries. Now to the question and, as an initial step, to a consideration of the Legion of Decency in this regard. Is the Legion of Decency a pressure group and, if so, are its pressures reprehensible?

I propose the consideration that the Legion is an "interest group" rather than a pressure group. This interpretation is certainly defensible if we follow, for instance, the reasoning of such a thinker in the social sciences as R. M. MacIver. According to his line of definition, "the tactics which are the essence of social pressures are intended not directly to change attitudes, but to control the behavior of recalcitrant or nonconforming individuals. . . . Pressure involves more than persuasion; it implies some kind of external inducement to limit or change the activities of others, ranging from direct or indirect economic inducement to ostracism, intimidation and violence. . . . A pressure group is defined by its techniques, an interest group by its objectives. A pressure group as such has no internal function but is directed outward, to the overcoming of resistance. Interests may be opposed but the relation of conflict is only one of the manifold relations they exhibit."[4]

Let us apply this description to the work of the Legion. If anything has emerged from our earlier description of the Legion, it should have been that the precise purpose of the Legion is to *change attitudes*; the attitudes, namely, of Catholics themselves toward the moral quality of the films they see. If the Catholic body at large does not first believe in and then

[4] In the *Encyclopedia of the Social Sciences*, Vol. XII, s.v. "Social Pressures," p. 347.

adhere to the Legion pledge (and it is a promise freely taken), then the Legion's work has failed or will. If Catholics are not convinced by the Legion that as a matter of ideal policy they ought certainly to stay away from C films and very probably, for the sake of the same noble ideal, from B films, then the Legion has not brought about an ennobling of Catholic ideals. The first purpose of the Legion is *not* "to control the behavior of recalcitrant or non-conforming individuals" (or groups); that is to say, in this instance, to bring the movie producers into line or to regiment the thinking of non-Catholics. Since, however, the very purpose of the Legion can be achieved only by *action*, the changed attitude it strives to foster can be shown only by an abstention from movies estimated as unworthy of Catholic viewing. It may fairly be said that the Legion would be magnificently achieving its goal simply if every Catholic in the United States did not attend C and B movies, even if such films continued to be shown in considerable numbers. Of course producers and exhibitors would not look smilingly on the loss of a Catholic audience running into the millions, and changes in the quality of films would come about, as they have, but that is the producers' worry, not the Legion's. The producers have put their wares before the "censorship of the market"; if they lose some of the market, the next move is up to them.

If this view—namely, that the Legion is an interest group rather than a pressure group—has validity enough to commend itself to thoughtful consideration by those who have not liked the campaign of the Legion, then we shall not have to delay long on the question whether the Legion uses the club of the boycott to achieve its ends. It is certain that the Legion does not employ any kind of secondary boycott; that is, it does not engage in any active efforts to enlist third parties (non-Catholics) in its campaign to shape the thinking of Catholics against attendance at undesirable films. If non-Catholic bodies (organized Protestant, Jewish, or civic groups) care to affirm their support of the Legion's ideals, their support would be heartily welcome. It was, as we shall see, twenty years ago.

As for this secondary boycott, from which the Legion must in all fairness be absolved, it may be good to give now the current legal thinking on this type of soliciting a withholding of patronage. According to one authority, though some states have forbidden secondary boycotts: "More recently judges have introduced the doctrine of unjustifiable cause and condemned those boycotts in which the primary or sole object was injury to another rather than advantage to themselves, or where the injury to one party did not carry with it corresponding or compensating advantage to the other."[5] Clearly, the primary purpose of the Legion is not "injury to another"; that is, to the film industry.

But does the Legion exercise a species of primary boycott—that is, "a refusal to patronize directed against the offending producer or exhibitor only"? Yes, for the simple reason that, in this specific field of raising Catholic taste and judgment in public entertainment, the immediate result will be and has to be, from the nature of the Legion's interest, a correlative distaste for the questionable films and, hence, abstention. The point about this type of boycott, however, is a fact that is never adverted to by those who use the word as though it were an automatic condemnation. That fact is simply that a primary boycott is not illegal, undemocratic, un-American, or "extra-legal," in the sense of just skirting the fringes of legality. "Courts have held that . . . mere withholding of patronage is not unlawful, and that the announcement or publication of such a purpose is *within the rights of those who agree together, even though it results in the injury of those against whom the acts are directed.*"[6] (Emphasis added.)

Let us sum up what seems to be a judicious estimate of the Legion of Decency as a "pressure group." There is sound reason for considering the Legion rather as an interest group. Since it does not actively enlist the support of "third parties" with the direct or sole purpose of injuring the offenders (producers and exhibitors), it does not engage in secondary boycott (illegal or otherwise); the primary boycott it simply cannot avoid because the interest it is engaged in fostering can show itself only through abstention.

These interpretations will certainly not be agreed to by all; they may seem to many a fine example of hairsplitting. But I

[5] Harry L. Laidler, *op. cit.*, p. 665.
[6] *Ibid.*

adduce this line of thought for the sober consideration of all Americans, Catholic or not, who feel, as I do, that organizations like the ACLU, the American Book Publishers Council, the Authors League, and others, ought to be extremely wary of pinning the tag of "undemocratic" or "un-American" on those with whom they disagree. I trust that some quiet thought along these lines will convince anyone of good will that the work of the Legion is wholly and soundly *in* the American tradition of free discussion, free criticism, free dissent.

It is harder to maintain the distinction between pressure and interest groups when we try to apply it to the NODL. This organization does indeed strive, as its very first and essential end, to change attitudes and, as such, may be called an interest group; but those changes are more directly brought about by coming to grips, as it were, with "recalcitrant" or "non-conformist" individuals than is or can be the case in the activities of the Legion of Decency. Hence the NODL does deserve far more than its brother organization the appellation of pressure group. The Legion aims directly at keeping Catholics away from immoral and degrading movies: the pressure (interest) is directed primarily at Catholics with the very probable consequence of a falling off of patronage and economic pressure on producer and distributor. The NODL, on the other hand, aims directly at removing the source of what it thinks to be the danger and, in so doing, brings pressure more immediately to bear on the vendor and, as a consequence, on the members of the community who may not agree on what is "objectionable" literature.

This being said, however, we must return again to the statement at the beginning of this chapter that the charge that such-and-such is a "pressure group" should never be allowed to blind us to the fact that such groups are by no means automatically proper objects of our democratic detestation. Neither the Legion nor the NODL would be in the least embarrassed by the charge that they are pressure groups were it not for the fact that in public and undisciplined thinking, fostered by the spirit of condemnation by epithet, "pressure group" has come to be identified with "fanatics," "bigots," and "extremists."

It would by no means give an adequate picture of the operations of pressure groups in the field of censorship if we did not turn a brief investigation on the anti-censorship group that is most vocal in combating both the Legion and the NODL. I dislike the task of harping on the ACLU, but I cannot avoid it, because of its prominence in the struggle. The question, then, naturally arises: Speaking of pressure groups, what of the ACLU?

It was in January of 1957 that the ACLU prepared and sent around for public support the famous "Statement" to which we have referred so often. This "Statement" was referred to in the press as "an attack" on the NODL. As mentioned earlier, some 168 authors, publishers, etc., joined in the attack, and the censorship problem, with special emphasis on Catholic activity, was in the public eye as it never had been before. Was this step in the ACLU's crusade against the NODL the work of a pressure group? I submit that when a miscellaneous group of people is asked to sign a statement on the ground that they are combating an "un-American" or "undemocratic" movement, they are being pressured by some slight fear and a considerably greater degree of desire for conformity. This is abundantly true when the group is made up largely of creative people: authors, playwrights, actors, and so on. We need look back no farther than the recent un-American activities investigations by our Congress to recall the good number of artists who had apparently signed just about anything that was said to be for "freedom," though the freedom professed turned out to be the Communist brand. Happily, it also turned out that a fair number of these signers were just good, ordinary (if slightly bemused) citizens who simply did not know what they were signing or could not see any further implications. The suspicion will not die that many of the signers of the ACLU's "Statement" are in the same category, pressured by fear of being different.

But there is more to the story than that. The ACLU's "Statement" was circulated thoroughly and the complete text, plus the signatures, was released to the press on May 6, 1957. But the ACLU was not yet in high gear. On July 6, 1957, Morris L. Ernst, prominent New York lawyer and one of the vice-chairmen of the ACLU, sent out over his signature a follow-up letter, which asked for contributions to a special fund. The fund was necessary, recipients were told, because "fighting what appears to be a well-entrenched and wealthy organization . . . namely an extremist group which is actively campaigning to have books of which *it* does not approve banned from libraries and bookstores . . . is costly." We have already alluded to the "loaded" words in Mr. Ernst's letter, and examination of the two words "well entrenched" and "wealthy" will disclose their pressure value and, incidentally, their lack of reality.

The two words reinforce one another. It is the wealthy man who is "well entrenched," and the suspicion is, when the words are used in conjunction, that he has to entrench himself well because there is some aura of suspicion about his wealth. We hardly speak of an honest day laborer being well entrenched in his financial position; we do so speak, or used to, at any rate, of the "robber barons." First of all, the NODL is not a "wealthy organization"; neither is the Legion. Their combined budgets are not one tenth of the ACLU's $278,-253.26 for fiscal 1955–56. When the ACLU generously offered to make available to its members the reprints of Monsignor Fitzgerald's article that had appeared in *America*, the NODL's Chicago office provided 38,500 for the ACLU to mail (the ACLU's 1955–56 membership was 29,903). The NODL's bulk mailings (mainly to Catholic parishes) range from 12,000 to 14,000; in addition, it has an indirect mailing list of some 1,300. The NODL has a central staff of the executive director, one part-time assistant, and one full-time secretary. The Legion's staff consists of the executive director and his assistant, both full time, and a full-time secretary. The ACLU's official letterhead lists thirty-three members on the Board of Directors and eighty National Committee members. In addition to Patrick Murphy Malin, the executive director, three assistant directors, an administrative assistant, a staff counsel, an advisor for international work, a membership secretary, and a director of the Washington office are catalogued.

I submit that, to the unbiased observer, it will seem that the ACLU is by far the wealthiest of the three organizations. Whether or not it is also "well entrenched" must be left to what one estimates the value of the ACLU's work to be. There is a distinction that must in all fairness be made here. Not all of the ACLU's funds go into the work of combating the "extremist" activities of the NODL. The ACLU fights the fight on many a front for the preservation and advancement of civil rights. How much of its total budget is earmarked for the struggle against the NODL, I have no way of knowing, but one would gather that the appeal for the special fund made in Mr. Ernst's letter will draw from the eager signers of the "Statement" contributions of some considerable proportions.

Once again I must allude to the basic misconception under which the ACLU and other similar organizations labor when they speak of "wealthy" organizations within the body of the Church. The NODL and the Legion do not have at their beck and call the corporate wealth of the Catholic Church in the United States. I suppose that if the headquarters of these two organizations were devastated by fire or ruined by rampant mobs, and if the diocese in which each is situated were not able to afford rebuilding, the bishops of the United States might all get together, and all school children be urged to contribute their pennies, and pulpits would resound with appeals —and the headquarters would rise from their ruins. But in ordinary circumstances the Legion and the NODL are given a modest annual subsidy and told to "make do" while making their own way. What "power" the Church is able to bring into being through the Legion and the NODL does not lie in their being "well-entrenched, wealthy" organizations but in the force of public opinion they are able to enlist for the moral betterment of the nation.

There is another aspect of pressure-group activity that brings us to a consideration of co-operation—or the lack of it.

In the ACLU's much-quoted "Statement," we read this sentence: "The NODL's instruction manual, while listing procedures for individual committees to conduct Parish Decency Crusades, invites the cooperation of non-Catholic groups in the organization of local Decent Literature Committees to carry on the NODL work; such cooperation has not thus far been wide-spread."

First of all, this playing down of co-operation slightly falsifies the picture. The NODL central office is in constant contact with numerous non-Catholic religious and civic groups.

All of this correspondence does not mean that the NODL's policies or procedures are approved or adopted, but at least these groups write in, not to excoriate the NODL for its "un-American" activities, but to inquire seriously and often anxiously about what can be done to rid the newsstands of the flood of filth. Subjoined is a list of such groups which have recently been in contact with the NODL. It will be noted that not all of them by any means are Catholic organizations.[7]

Be this as it may about the present state of co-operation between the NODL and other groups, the question arises about why the ACLU seems so complacent that there is not "widespread" co-operation at present. The answer, from the ACLU's viewpoint, is of course obvious and immediate: the less co-operation there is with an "extremist" group that is fundamentally "un-American," the better. But suppose, for the sake of the argument, that this book has by now shaken one's conviction that the NODL *is* justly tarred with that brush. Then one might begin to wonder if more co-operation would not be a good thing. A glimpse into the past will reveal that there was indeed a great deal of co-operation before the

[7] Newport (R.I.) Citizens' Committee on Literature, Inc.; Citizens' Committee for Decent Literature, Joliet, Ill.; Decent Literature Committee, Camden, W. Va.; Decent Literature Council, Coral Gables, Fla.; Muhlenberg Township Parent-Teacher Ass'n., Laureldale, Pa.; City of Poughkeepsie's Committee on Questionable Literature, Poughkeepsie, N.Y.; Parent-Teachers' Association, Kalamazoo, Mich.; Committee on Decent Literature, Stevens Point, Wis.; Committee for Clean Literature, Corpus Christi, Tex.; Committee for Decent Literature, Exchange Club, Orlando, Fla.; Organization for Clean Publications, Williamsport, Pa.; Springfield Church Group for Promotion of Decent Literature, Springfield, Vt.; Wyandotte Civic Organization for Decent Literature, Wyandotte, Mich.; Mount Clemens Civic Committee for Decent Literature, Mount Clemens, Mich.; River Rouge Committee for Decent Literature, River Rouge, Mich.; Mayor's Clean Literature Committee, Borough of Rutherford, N.Y.; Literature Review Committee of Chatham County, Ga.; Advisory Board on Objectionable Publications to the Government of the Province of Alberta, Canada; Georgia Literature Commission; Women's Civic League, Hills, Minn.; Mayor's Committee on Decent Literature, Burlington, Ia.; Clean Comics Committee of the Lancaster County Community Council, Lancaster, Pa.; United Citizens' Committee for Decent Literature, Carlstadt and East Rutherford, N.Y.; Advisory Committee on Literature for Youth, Westfield, N.Y.

epithets "un-American" and "undemocratic" began to obfuscate the issues at stake. The instances of approval and co-operation that will follow refer explicitly to the Legion of Decency, not to the NODL, but the general principle involved is the same.

The Legion was just getting under way in 1933 when it began to be clear not only that it would get wide co-operation from other religious groups but that, in fact, some such groups were already on record as advocating the kind of campaign that the Legion would take up and push to a resounding success. In 1934, for instance, Bishop John F. Noll of Fort Wayne, a member of the newly appointed (Catholic) Episcopal Committee on Motion Pictures, wrote:

"There exists a Federal Motion Picture Council in America, Inc., whose slogan is 'Mobilize for Wholesome Motion Pictures.' This Council is constituted almost entirely of non-Catholics, and as General Secretary, the Reverend Scheafe Chase is soliciting Catholic cooperation for the passage of the Patman Bill—designed to secure Federal supervision of motion pictures 'at the source of production, before they are filmed, and for the prohibition of blind and block booking' . . .

"Within the writer's own diocese Protestants of several cities have set Catholics an example by securing pledges from their people to remain away from the theatre until it desists from serving filth."[8]

Almost at the same time, Archbishop John T. McNicholas, O.P., of Cincinnati, then chairman of the Episcopal Committee, wrote in even wider terms:

"It is very heartening to realize that an awakening is taking place. From all sections of the country, from all groups—Protestant, Jew and those affiliated with no organized religion, and from countless Catholics—comes the word that the movement against immoral cinema was too long delayed. It has not been possible to acknowledge all the communications expressing this thought which were sent to the members of the Episcopal Committee. . . .

[8] *American Ecclesiastical Review*, Vol. 90 (1934), pp. 367–69. As we remarked above, the Catholic stand was against any such federal censorship.

"Non-Catholics in every section, men of every profession have spoken words of encouragement and have expressed their wish to cooperate. . . ."[9]

But there was much more co-operation than this type that was singled out by the prelates, who might have been thought to be speaking *pro domo sua.*

"The New York *Times,* between June and November of the campaign year, gave forty reports on Protestant activity, mentioning twenty-seven different groups or leaders of groups. An incomplete list compiled from the *Times, America,* and the diocesan reports of the Episcopal Committee contain the names of fifty-four organizations of Protestant or Jewish churches, ministers and rabbis who cooperated in securing pledges, or publicly announced their support of the Legion campaign. The organizations range from local ministerial groups, through city, state and regional councils or federations of churches, to the Federal Council of the Churches of Christ in America.

"It is altogether impossible to give a numerical estimate of the effect of this activity upon the enrollment of the members in the Legion of Decency. Dr. Tippy, as head of the Department of Church and Social Service of the Federal Council of the Churches of Christ in America, announced at one state of the campaign that Protestants were signing pledges sent out by his organization 'by hundreds of thousands.' "[10]

As examples of the reaction of the secular press, as distinguished from the simple reporting of the reaction of non-Catholic groups, we may quote the following two excerpts:

"In a calm and impartial yet serious discussion of the question, Cardinal Hayes calls the attention of all the Catholic priests in the Archdiocese of New York to the campaign tak-

[9] *Idem.,* Vol. 91 (1934), pp. 114–17.

[10] This is taken from a thesis by Reverend Paul W. Facey, S.J., "The Legion of Decency: A Sociological Analysis of the Emergence and Development of a Social Pressure Group," p. 61. This doctoral dissertation, prepared in the Department of Political Philosophy at Fordham University, New York, has not been published. Father Facey's documentation and analysis supply most of the material for the first part of an article, "The Legion of Decency," by John C. Ford, S.J., and Gerald Kelly, S.J., in the September issue of *Theological Studies* (Woodstock, Md.), referred to above, p. 89.

ing form under the name of the Legion of Decency. He brings no railing accusations against the film industry in all its activities. What he singles out for condemnation is the 'evil character and shocking debasement of many motion pictures.' The Cardinal fully admits the opportunity of motion pictures to exercise a most potent and refining influence. But they have largely missed it. The stirring within the Catholic Church against productions that openly and flagrantly offend is not due to a narrow ascetic outlook upon life. . . . But the Catholic Church, in common with Protestants and Jews . . . sees the need of uniting to protect children from moral defilement. This is the sum and substance of the indictment."[11]

In like manner the Springfield (Mass.) *Union* spoke up:

"The movement against debasing motion pictures inaugurated by the Roman Catholic Bishops through the Legion of Decency . . . is drawing strong support from the Federal Council of Churches and other Protestant groups. One does not readily recall a crusade like this which so quickly solidified into one front Catholic and Protestant sentiment concerning public morals. Other religious bodies, such as Hebrew congregations, are showing marked sympathy with the purpose of the more numerous sects. Thus far the movement is notable for the absence of a demand for censorship statutes. It contemplates a purely private, voluntary drive involving agreements or pledges of non-patronage of theatres showing debasing films. . . . There is no new law to be enforced by the police. 'Personal liberty' will not be more crucified than hitherto by stage censors to arouse the antagonism of the embattled libertarians. . . ."[12]

Even more startling to today's reader is the following statement from the *Christian Century*:

"It has been heartening to see the Protestant reaction to the launching of the Catholic crusade. Seldom has there been

[11] New York *Times*, editorial, "Evil Motion Pictures," June 13, 1934.

[12] In an editorial, "The Legion of Decency," July 9, 1934. The editorial goes on to predict that the widespread non-Catholic co-operation with the Legion will have "an electrical effect" on the motion-picture studios. Whoever wrote the editorial was gifted with the charism of at least minor prophecy.

as clear an illustration of the essential unity of purpose of the religious bodies in the realm of social and moral action. . . . Thousands of Protestant ministers and laity . . . say: 'Thank God that the Catholics are at last opening up on this foul thing as it deserves! What can we do to help?' "[13]

A general conclusion to be drawn from all this co-operation is:

". . . Non-Catholic leaders and their followers encouraged the Catholic leaders and followers of the Legion to be vigorous and unyielding in the pursuit of their objectives, by demonstrating to this minority group that many others shared their aims. Furthermore, the non-Catholic support made it impossible for the industry to defy the Catholic demands, or to turn them aside with the expectation that the non-Catholic majority would refuse to support the Catholic minority."[14]

Whatever the co-operation that now exists between the Legion and the NODL and non-Catholic religious groups and civic organizations, it is quite obviously nowhere near as close and universal as it was twenty years ago. Why? What has happened? Perhaps it will be said that non-Catholic co-operation cooled because the Legion got more and more "dictatorial," or that non-Catholics realized almost too late that they were aligned with a "pressure group." But certainly a study of the history of the Legion will show that it wielded more "power" in its early days than it does now. If we may put it so, the Legion has mellowed with the years, and the same aging process may be reasonably expected with the NODL. The point is that it really ought to be easier to co-operate now with these two organizations than in the past. But there is not as much co-operation, and the ACLU rejoices over the widening chasm.

The point I should like to raise for mutual consideration, and in no sense as a charge that I am prepared to substantiate with chapter and verse, is this: Has the ACLU (and other similar pressure groups) helped to widen the chasm, or do its activities in the field of censorship merely reflect the chasm that has yawned because of other causes?

[13] June 20, 1934, pp. 822 ff. Facey, *op. cit.*, p. 61.
[14] Facey, *op. cit.*, p. 58.

No one will deny that there are Catholic-Protestant tensions working in our land today to disrupt a sense of common moral responsibility—"the essential unity of purpose of the religious bodies in the realm of social and moral action," as the *Christian Century* aptly put it two decades ago. One of the fields of this tension is precisely that of censorship, and I am afraid it must be said that the ACLU is happy to screw the tensions up to the screaming point. As Father Murray remarked in his *America* article, this is all too frequently the pattern in American debate on public issues, especially those that touch on public morality:

"Thus the argument [between the NODL and, in this case, Mr. Fischer of *Harper's*] fulfills the customary American pattern. The next step is for the contestants to retire from the field, either in sorrow or in anger or in both. Thereafter their partisans move in. Epithets are bandied; labels are exchanged; *non-sequitur's* proliferate. Until finally, both sides mutter disgustedly, 'So's your old man.' And there is, for a time, a sullen silence."[15]

In the censorship debate we seem now to have reached the point of the epithet, the labels, and the *non sequiturs*. And I cannot help feeling that it is precisely the labels of "undemocratic," and so on, stuck upon the NODL and the Legion that have frightened away very much of the co-operation that was evident in the thirties and is, I am convinced, latent now. But what religious or civic group will now dare make common cause with the NODL when it is a well-known fact (if "often repeated" means "well known") that the NODL is an "extremist" clique with which not even all Catholics agree?

A further danger arises from ACLU pressure-group tactics. The only thing that makes the NODL a thorn in the side for many who disagree with it is that its operations dare to impinge on others than Catholics in our pluralistic society. If the NODL (and the Legion, of course) would speak only to Catholics and be able to restrict their influence so that it reached nobody but Catholics, neither the ACLU nor any other anti-censorship group would, they maintain, have any objection in the wide world. But this is obviously impossible,

15 November 3, 1956, p. 121.

for Catholics in the United States live and work and discuss and play in a pluralistic society, and some of their attitudes, thoughts, and convictions are bound, as it were, to spill over. So, for all practical purposes, what the ACLU and others devoutly wish is not merely that these two Catholic "censorship" organizations would talk only to themselves but actually that they would not talk at all, for there is always the danger that they may be overheard.

To make no bones about it, then, my charge is simply this: The ACLU and similar groups are engaged in a campaign to censor the Legion and the NODL out of existence by disagreeing with their right to disagree and putting their own criticism on a phony basis of "Americanism." This is a serious charge and I do not make it for the fun of the thing. I make it because it raises a crucial problem of discussion in any pluralistic society. Walter Lippmann is concerned with this problem when he writes:

"For in the absence of debate unrestricted utterance leads to the degradation of opinion. By a kind of Gresham's law the more rational is overcome by the less rational, and the opinions that will prevail will be those which are held most ardently by those with the most passionate will. For that reason the freedom to speak can never be maintained merely by objecting to interference with the liberty of the press, of printing, of broadcasting, of the screen. It can be maintained only by promoting debate.

"In the end what men will most ardently desire is to suppress those who disagree with them, and, therefore, stand in the way of the realization of their desires. Thus, once confrontation in debate is no longer necessary, the toleration of all opinions leads to intolerance. Freedom of speech, separate from its essential principle, leads through a short transitional chaos to the destruction of freedom of speech.

"It follows, I believe, that in the practice of freedom of speech, the degree of toleration that will be maintained is directly related to the effectiveness of the confrontation in debate which prevails or can be organized."[16]

[16] *The Public Philosophy* (Boston: Little, Brown, 1955), pp. 129–30.

There has been to date very little confrontation in debate between the ACLU, the American Book Publishers Association, the Authors League, and others on the one hand and the Legion of Decency and the NODL on the other. There has been debate of a kind in various articles and statements. Perhaps it may turn out to be the sole contribution of this book that it eased the way for such confrontation that may bring more light and less heat into the controversy.

There is one final point, and the argument that seeks to establish it may seem to be fetched from afar. But it is a most basic point, and I am afraid that little more can be done here than to suggest it for future discussion at more capable hands. It seems to me that the type of thinking that underlies many of the attacks on the Legion and the NODL strikes quite directly at the principle of subsidiarity in social and political life. That principle, to put it briefly, says that if a less complex social group can handle a specific problem, no more complex group should step in to do the job. If a family, for instance, can provide for its own health, it should do so and not immediately run to its city's visiting-nurse association or public-welfare assistance. If a city can maintain its own streets and sewage, it ought not to call on state aid; if a state can keep up its own highways, it should not cry for federal funds, and so on. Of course, especially in our technical age, there are many projects that can be carried out only by state, let us say, or federal know-how and funds. But the principle still remains true, and it is a fundamental one from which springs much of the vitality of a democratic society.

Further, this principle of subsidiarity is enshrined in Catholic social thought. It was given perhaps its most pithy expression in Pius XI's encyclical, *Quadragesimo Anno* ("Forty Years After")—after, that is, the encyclical *Rerum Novarum* ("On the Conditions of the Working Classes") by Leo XIII:

"The supreme authority of the State ought . . . to let subordinate groups handle matters and concerns of lesser importance which would otherwise dissipate its efforts greatly. Thereby the State will more freely, powerfully and effectively do all those things which belong to it alone because it alone can do them: directing, watching, urging, restraining, as occasion requires and necessity demands. Therefore, those in com-

mand should be sure that the more perfectly a graduated
order is preserved among the various associations, in observance of the principle of 'subsidiary function,' the stronger
social authority and effectiveness will be, and the happier and
more prosperous the condition of the State."[17]

This principle of "subsidiary function" applies, of course, in
its primary meaning to larger issues and more socially important groups than either the ACLU or the NODL. Its most
obvious validity and challenge is in the field of the relation of
labor and government, of federal and local government, and
so on. But the spirit of subsidiarity and the ideal it proposes
work down to all levels of society, even to the family. If
mother and father, for instance, let John and Jane do for themselves what they can and ought to do, instead of trying to live
the children's lives for them, we would have fewer problem
children—and problem parents.

In this matter of censorship we can apply, it seems to me,
the same principle. Law is without doubt the last recourse for
the solution of many social problems, and our first chapter
on authority and the nature of the coercive aspect of law may
have made clear that Catholics, no less than anyone else (perhaps even more), are committed to respect for law and readi-
ness to welcome its necessary intervention. But in one sense
law is the *last* resort. If social problems and conflicts can be
solved without recourse to law, though never in violation of
either the letter or spirit of the law, they ought to be so solved.
I could doubtless, though after some vexing delay, solve the
problem of where my property ends and my neighbor's begins
by going directly to the courts; but perhaps if I talked it over
with my neighbor we might come to a speedier and certainly
a friendlier solution.

I think the tendency of the ACLU and others to work on
the assumption that *only* the law can settle censorship cases
is a tendency to run to mother's apron strings. It is a drift toward abdicating local autonomy; toward calling in the bigger
organization to settle a problem that might well be brought

[17] This quotation and the entire encyclical may be readily found
in *The Church and the Reconstruction of the Modern World*, ed. by
Reverend Terence McLaughlin (Garden City, N.Y.: Image Books,
1957), p. 247.

to amicable solution by the smaller contending parties. It is, in brief, a drift toward "big government," toward another step in the establishment of the "welfare state."

These are big words applied to a problem that is, after all, not quite so pressing as racial integration, to take an example. But the censorship debate, if this analysis of it is sound, does entail much more than merely the problem of whether Johnny will or will not read this lascivious magazine. If the censorship problem does not directly impinge on the problem of civil rights, as ACLU and others think it does, it does impinge on the problem, perhaps even more basic, of civic-mindedness. The American Catholics who stay away from *Baby Doll* and the American Catholics who go about urging the news vendors and bookstall proprietors to get rid of some of the more suggestive literature are doing so not just because "the Church" motivates them but because they are interested in a morally and culturally better United States.

It is by no means drawing the longbow to assert that *the* Catholic viewpoint on censorship is an admirably sane adjustment of the sometimes divergent drives of law and freedom, and that the viewpoint of American Catholics is truly a democratic viewpoint, for it has confidence first in the ability of people to work at their own immediate problems and second in the probability that, when viewpoints differ, Mr. Lippmann's "confrontation" can solve most problems.

Writing in the *Encyclopedia of the Social Sciences*, Harold D. Lasswell provides a thought with which I shall end this section; it also makes some suggestions that may be practical:

"In a certain sense the 'philosophy of compromise' is in itself a curb on the tendency to resort to coercion rather than discussions; but from another point of view it is fatalistic and negativistic, for it seems to concede in advance that there is no truly inclusive set of social aims in relation to which local differences may be reconciled. . . . In some quarters, the philosophy of compromise has tended to pass over into a 'philosophy of integration.' The solution of a conflict by integration is a redefinition of the interests involved; the parties cannot identify their 'wins and losses.' Such a concept is affirmative and challenging, for it dares suggest that no social conflict is so serious that creative intelligence may not . . . resolve it."[18]

I firmly believe that there is enough "creative intelligence" in both the ACLU and NODL—let us specify these two antagonists as merely representative of the two sides in the debate—to get together for a reconsideration of their stands, a redefinition of the terms of the conflict. I believe there is possible a co-operation in which both sides, without abandoning their principles a whit, may still come to pool the viewpoints on which they can agree and minimize the frictions that occur when and where they differ.

In his article in *America*, Erik von Kuehnelt-Leddihn has these provocative two paragraphs:

"Imagine you arrive in Heidelberg, a German university town. You study the bulletin board of a Catholic church and see a list of the locally shown movies and their ratings. If you happen to look at the notices of the neighboring Evangelical church, you will see the same list with the same ratings. A strange coincidence? By no means. In Heidelberg a joint interfaith committee gives advice about the films.

"Two hours later you stand before the Cathedral in Frankfurt, where the Holy Roman Emperors were crowned. There you will find another list, with criticisms or recommendations, but without classification. It has been prepared by a civic committee."

Co-operation between religious groups, the welcome assistance of civic groups, a general desire to express unity of common outlook on this particular problem of public morality are obviously strongly at work in Europe in the evaluation of motion pictures. It may be extremely naïve, to say the least, to suggest, as an ending to our consideration of censorship, that some such co-operation can actually come about in this country. The suggestion will nevertheless be made.

The rock-bottom foundation for this suggestion—or, if you will, plea—that avenues leading toward co-operation be mutually explored is the existence of good will on both sides to the controversy. There is no need to underline the sorry fact that there is probably some ill will too. But I know that the

18 *Loc. cit.*, Vol. IV, s.v. "Social Conflict," pp. 195–96.

directors of the Legion and the NODL do not feel that the
officials of the ACLU and the other anti-censorship groups are
fiendishly trying to debauch the morals of the American public. They may feel that such officials, in their passionate devotion to civil rights, are inclined to soft-pedal civil obligations, but they do not feel that obscenity is being defended
for its own sake. And certainly the rank and file of U.S. Catholic citizens who back the Legion and the NODL do not think
that the non-Catholic citizenry of the United States is a morally irresponsible mass. On the other hand, it can be safely
asserted, I trust, that the officials of the ACLU and other
organizations do not believe that the Legion and the NODL
directors are consciously trying to undermine our American
democracy, despite the sweeping nature of some of the
charges.

Accordingly, naïve as it may seem, I start with the assumption that there is good will on both sides. Unfortunately it is
good will that is untapped. The day may be long in coming
when we shall have the co-operation manifest in Mr. Kuehnelt-Leddihn's report, but a start has to be made if we are
not willing to settle for the situation in which, as Father
Murray complained, each side mutters, "So's your old man,"
and retires—not into sullen silence—but into more vociferous
charge and countercharge.

As a first suggestion, at which I have hinted above, would
it not be possible in future debates in the public press to
abstain from the use of the word "censorship"? Since the
ACLU claims that the NODL, let us say, does "censor" and
the NODL flatly says it doesn't, the use of the word is really
meaningless. The word "control" would be much more accurate and would be relieved of the hysterical overtones by now
connected with "censorship." Second, if we could determine
to avoid the "loaded" words, such as "pressure group," on the
one hand, and "defenders of poison," on the other, the atmosphere might clear a bit. Third, if scrupulous accuracy would
be maintained in the descriptions of each other's purposes and
practices, each side would get a clearer picture of the other.
At this point all I can protest in my own favor is that I have
tried to be fair and accurate in such descriptions.

But further, is no practical joint action imaginable? What

might the results be if, say, once or twice a year a representative of the American Civil Liberties Union, of the Legion of Decency, of the American Booksellers Council, of the National Office for Decent Literature, of the Authors League, of the American Library Association, and so on, sat around a table for a day's or a three-day conference, discussing mutual concerns and amicably trying to reach "integration" of their problems? And what might be some common ground from which they could start? There is, for one thing, the problem I mentioned above of the *availability* of the debatable printed material. Could not such a joint meeting come up with some recommendations to our lawmakers on the problem of "controlling" the distributors of such material? Perhaps some steps might be considered toward putting into practice in this country England's scheme of not allowing unattended children to enter movie theatres showing adult films. Theatre owners would, of course, be up in arms at such a suggestion, but they would be much less armed if the scheme were presented by a joint committee than if it were proposed by Catholic groups alone.

There are other terrains of mutual concern and interest which such a joint meeting could open up far sooner and more fruitfully than I am equipped to. And the fact of such a meeting need not—indeed, could not—entail on either side a retreat from principle. The philosophy of law and freedom which underlies the Catholic position need not be endorsed by the non-Catholic participants; the Catholics present would not abandon their adherence to those bases. But certainly both share the mutual American concern of the betterment of our cultural and moral life under the protection of our constitutional freedom. If a group of intelligent and devoted American citizens cannot discuss with benefit such a mutual concern, then we are indeed leagues away from the "confrontation" that Mr. Lippmann considers so essential for the preservation of our democratic way of life.

There is a famous phrase that has been much overworked, but I would crave the indulgence of the reader to put it into harness again. It is attributed to St. Augustine, and its direct application is to debates among Catholic theologians on ramifications and implications in the Christian revelation. But, without straining the point, the phrase can be applied to the touchy field of censorship. The pro-censorship and the anti-censorship factions would find themselves closer to a "confrontation" if they would each take as their slogan: *In necesariis, unitas; in dubiis, libertas; in omnibus, caritas.* "In essentials, unity"—we can stand united on the essentials of upholding public morals in an atmosphere of freedom. "In debatable matters, liberty"—lack of agreement need not, must not, entail the imputation of base motives. "In all things, charity or love" —whether we agree or disagree, we do so as children of our common Father, God.

I hope that it will have been evident to the reader that the effort was made to write this book in the spirit of that phrase.

APPENDICES

The Harm Good People Do*

JOHN FISCHER

A little band of Catholics is now conducting a shocking attack on the rights of their fellow citizens. They are engaged in an un-American activity which is as flagrant as anything the Communist party ever attempted—and which is, in fact, very similar to Communist tactics. They are harming their country, their Church, and the cause of freedom.

Their campaign is particularly dangerous because few people realize what they are up to. It can hurt you—indeed, it already has—without your knowing it. It is spreading rapidly but quietly; and so far no effective steps have been taken to halt it.

Even the members of this organization probably do not recognize the damage they are doing. They are well-meaning people, acting from deeply moral impulses. They are trying, in a misguided way, to cope with a real national problem, and presumably they think of themselves as patriots and servants of the Lord. Perhaps a majority of Americans, of all faiths, would sympathize with their motives—though not with their methods.

They do not, of course, speak for all Catholics. On the contrary, they are defying the warnings of some of their Church's most respected teachers and theologians. The Catholic Church as a whole certainly cannot be blamed for their actions, any more than it could be held responsible a generation ago for the political operations of Father Coughlin.

* Copyright, 1956, by Harper & Brothers. Reprinted from *Harper's Magazine* by special permission.

This group calls itself the National Organization for Decent Literature. Its headquarters are in Chicago; its director is the Very Reverend Monsignor Thomas Fitzgerald. Its main purpose is to make it impossible for anybody to buy books and other publications which it does not like. Among them are the works of some of the most distinguished authors now alive—for example, winners of the Nobel Prize, the Pulitzer Prize, and the National Book Award.

Its chief method is to put pressure on news dealers, drug stores, and booksellers, to force them to remove from their stocks every item on the NODL blacklist. Included on this list are reprint editions of books by Ernest Hemingway, William Faulkner, John Dos Passos, George Orwell, John O'Hara, Paul Hyde Bonner, Emile Zola, Arthur Koestler, and Joyce Cary. In some places—notably Detroit, Peoria, and the suburbs of Boston—the organization has enlisted the local police to threaten booksellers who are slow to "co-operate."[1]

This campaign of intimidation has no legal basis. The books so listed have not been banned from the mails, and in the overwhelming majority of cases no legal charges have ever been brought against them. Indeed, it seems that the National Organization for Decent Literature deliberately prefers to ignore the established legal channels for proceedings against books which it thinks improper. Its chosen weapons are boycott and literary lynching.

For example, early last year committees of laymen from Catholic churches in the four northern counties of New Jersey —Union, Hudson, Essex, and Bergen—began to call on local merchants. These teams were armed with the NODL lists. They offered "certificates," to be renewed each month, to those storekeepers who would agree to remove from sale all of the listed publications. To enforce their demands, they warned the merchants that their parishioners would be advised to patronize only those stores displaying a certificate.

---

[1] In his letter of January, 1961, referred to above, Monsignor Fitzgerald states that shortly after the publication of Mr. Fischer's charge he "checked on the various places that Mr. Fischer mentioned, where, allegedly, NODL groups were bringing police pressure to bear upon local distributors and retailers. There was not one case where I could find substantiating evidence of this fact."

Contact, a bulletin published by the Sacred Heart Parish Societies of Orange, New Jersey, listed fourteen merchants in its March 1955 issue. "The following stores," it said, "have agreed to co-operate with the Parish Decency Committee in not displaying or selling literature disapproved by the National Organization for Decent Literature. . . . Please patronize these stores only. They may be identified by the certificate which is for one month only."

Similar tactics have been followed in scores of other communities. Even in Nevada—a state not noted for Puritanical temper—the Council of Catholic Men has asked booksellers to purge from their shelves a list of books which included such widely read novels as *Mr. Roberts* and *From Here to Eternity*. When an Associated Press reporter pointed out that millions of people already were familiar with these works, in print and on film, the state chairman of the campaign, Paul Laxalt of Carson City, replied:

"We've got to stand by the list. If we make one exception the list would be chopped up."

Such tactics are highly effective. Most news dealers, druggists, and similar merchants carry paper-bound books only as a minor side line. Moreover, they receive from the wholesalers more books than they have space for; if they remove one title from their racks, there are plenty of others to take its place. They don't want trouble. It is never good business to argue with a customer—so most of them readily comply with this form of private censorship. After all, their other customers, who might want to read a book by Faulkner or Hemingway or Zola, will never know that it has been suppressed, and when they don't find it on the shelves they probably will buy something else.

For these reasons it was possible for the Archdiocesan Council of Catholic Men in St. Louis to report recently that it had "obtained the consent of about one-third of the store owners approached in a campaign to ask merchants to submit to voluntary screening. . . ."

Something—but not much—can be said in defense of the National Organization for Decent Literature and its local campaigners. A good many tawdry and disreputable magazines, paper-bound reprints, and comic books have been offered for sale on a lot of newsstands. A few publishers unquestionably have tried to base their sales appeal on sex and violence; the pictures and text on the covers of their publications often hint that the contents are far more salacious than they are in fact. (Such misrepresentation, however, is less common now than it was a few years ago, and both the contents and the covers of most pocket-size books seem to be growing less lurid.)

It can be argued, too, that law enforcement agencies in some cities have not been vigorous in enforcing the statutes against obscene publications. Finally, the "decent literature" campaigners apparently feel that their main mission is to protect young people, whose judgment is unformed and who might be attracted to sleazy reading matter by a provocative newsstand display; they seem to take far less interest in the hard-bound editions of the same books available in libraries or regular book stores. The Detroit NODL, for example, states that its list is "not intended as a restrictive list for adults"—though it does not explain how adults could purchase the books if merchants have been persuaded not to stock them.

But the motives of these zealous people are not the issue. The real issue is whether any private group—however well-meaning—has a right to dictate what other people may read.

Clearly any church, or any sub-group within a church, has a right to advise its own members about their reading matter.

Clearly, too, anybody has a right to try to *persuade* other people to read or to refrain from reading anything he sees fit.

The National Organization for Decent Literature, however, goes much further. Its campaign is not aimed at Catholics alone, and it is not attempting to *persuade* readers to follow its views. It is *compelling* readers, of all faiths, to bow to its dislikes, by denying them a free choice in what they buy.[2]

---

[2] No doubt unconsciously, the Catholic War Veterans, Our Lady of Sorrows Post No. 1046, underlined the similarity between these tactics and those of the Communists. In a February 25, 1956, mailing to book dealers in Hartford, Connecticut, it enclosed the NODL list of "objectionable" publications—and it quoted the Chinese Communists who have been conducting a campaign of their own against "objectionable" literature:

" 'These books and pictures seriously harm those workers who by constantly looking at them can easily become degenerate in their

This principle is of course unacceptable to Catholics—as it is to all Americans—if they take the trouble to think about it for a moment. How would Catholics react if, say, a group of Jewish laymen were to threaten merchants with boycott unless they banned from their shops all publications which referred to the divinity of Christ? Some religious denominations believe that gambling is immoral; most Catholics do not, and many of their parishes raise considerable sums by means of bingo games and raffles. What if some Protestant sect were to try to clean out of the stores all publications which spoke tolerantly of gambling, and to boycott every merchant who bought a raffle ticket?

The principle at stake was set forth with admirable clarity by Father John Courtney Murray, S.J., professor of moral theology at Woodstock College, Maryland, in a recent address on "Literature and Censorship." He listed four rules, which ought to command the enthusiastic support of all Americans regardless of religious belief:

(1) "Each minority group has the right to censor for its own members, if it so chooses, the contents of the various media of communication, and to protect them, by means of its own choosing, from materials considered harmful according to its standards." (He also pointed out that in the United States "all religious groups . . . are minority groups.")

(2) "No minority group has the right to demand that government should impose a general censorship" on material "judged to be harmful according to the special standards held within one group."

(3) "Any minority group has the right to work toward the elevation of standards of public morality . . . through the use of the methods of persuasion and pacific argument."

(4) "No minority group has the right to impose its own religious or moral views on other groups, through the use of methods of force, coercion, or violence."

---

thinking,' cautions the *Peking Worker's Daily* as quoted by *Newsweek* magazine, January 23, 1956. We have to hand it to the Communists . . . who have launched a nationwide campaign against pornographic trash. . . . Should not this example provoke a similar literary clean-up in our land where the morality of our actions is gauged by service to God and not to an atheistic state?"

And Father Murray went on to warn that methods of coercion are especially imprudent for Catholic associations.

"The chief danger," he said, "is lest the Church itself be identified in the public mind as a power-association. The identification is injurious; it turns into hatred of the faith. And it has the disastrous effect of obscuring from the public view the true visage of the Church as God's kingdom of truth and freedom, justice and love."

He quoted from Jacques Leclercq "of the Catholic University of Louvain, who is no slight authority" the dictum that "no government has ever succeeded in finding a balanced policy of combating unhealthy sexual propaganda without injuring legitimate freedom or provoking other equally grave or worse disorders."

Finally, Father Murray emphasized that "censorship in the civil order must be a judicial process," carried out under the statutes and according to the due processes of law.

The conclusions which flow from Father Murray's teachings seem plain enough:

(1) *For the National Organization for Decent Literature.* It should stop immediately its campaign of threats, blacklisting, and boycott. It should then pursue its aims by the legitimate methods of persuasion, propaganda, and action through the courts. Most states have adequate laws against the publication and sale of indecent literature. In cases where the law seems inadequate, the legislature can be persuaded to amend it, by the normal means of lobbying and petition. In cases where the law is not enforced, public officials should certainly be reminded of their duty—and opposed at the polls, in the democratic way, if they fall down on their jobs.

Above all, the NODL ought to consider the possibility of guiding young readers by positive rather than negative techniques. Youngsters are not likely to read trash whenever they have good books readily available. If they are brought up in homes where good literature is a constant part of their environment—where parents read to them from infancy, and encourage them to build up their own libraries—then there is scant chance that they will be attracted by comics or two-bit horrors.

What has the NODL done to urge parents to give their

children such basic moral training? Has it done all it can to foster topnotch libraries—public, school, church, and family? In how many communities has it sponsored campaigns to stimulate good reading?

(2) *For news dealers, booksellers, and other merchants.* They should muster the courage to defy any group of private citizens which tries to impose its own brand of censorship on the publications they offer for sale. And, with equal courage, they should set their own house in order; they should refuse to sell any publication which—in their own untrammeled judgment—falls below their own standards as responsible business men.

(3) *For the patriotic citizen.* He should protest against the lynching of books just as vigorously as against the lynching of people. He should go out of his way to support the merchants who resist such coercion. He should point out to the members of the National Organization for Decent Literature (and to any other self-appointed censors in his community) the immeasurable damage they are doing to the American way of life, to the very foundations of democratic government.

For the gravest harm done here is not to the Catholic Church—though as Father Murray noted, that is dangerous enough—or to the individual who is denied the right to choose his own books. The great peril is to the fabric of orderly government. It is always injured when any group takes the law into its own hands. And whenever such a band of vigilantes succeeds in imposing its will by force, some other—and perhaps more sinister—group is encouraged to try the same thing.

Dean Joseph O'Meara of the Notre Dame Law School recently put it like this:

"Unfortunately many sincere people do not comprehend the genius of our democracy . . . such people would deny free speech to those with whom they are in fundamental disagreement. . . . They would establish a party line in America—*their* party line, of course. This is an alien concept, a totalitarian concept; it is not consonant with the American tradition; it is anti-democratic; it is, in short, subversive and it should be recognized for what it is."

Still another eminent Catholic—Senator Joseph Kennedy of

Massachusetts—summed up the case in even more prophetic terms.

"The lock on the door of the legislature, the parliament, or the assembly hall," he said, "by order of the King, the Commissar, or the Führer—has historically been followed or preceded by a lock on the door of the printer's, the publisher's, or the bookseller's."

The Bad Arguments Intelligent Men Make*

REV. JOHN COURTNEY MURRAY, S.J.

From his "Editor's Easy Chair" (*Harper's*, October 1956) John Fischer looks out and sees "immeasurable damage" being done "to the American way of life and to the very foundations of democratic government." This has become a familiar vision; many of us share it. But we frequently differ on the question, who or what is doing the damage?

In Mr. Fischer's view the damage is being done by "a little band of Catholics" who are "conducting a shocking attack on the rights of their fellow citizens" through the medium of an organization called the National Organization for Decent Literature, which undertakes to "censor" certain publications.

I take a rather broader view. I see a large band of people, of all faiths, who are conducting a shocking attack on the reason of their fellow citizens through the medium of passionately irrational argument about important public issues. I believe that nothing is more damaging to democracy than lack of rationality in public argument. The foundations of our society are indeed laid in an identifiable consensus. But they are more importantly laid in a reasonable disposition to argue our many disagreements in intelligent and temperate fashion, using restrained language, avoiding misstatements, overstatements or simplifications, and endeavoring to define issues with precision in the light of all the relevant principles and facts. I believe that whatever corrupts rational public argument corrupts democracy.

* Reprinted from *America* by special permission.

It has seemed to me that censorship is one of the public issues that are being deformed by bad argument, emanating from all sides. Hence on May 4, 1956, in a talk given before the Thomas More Association in Chicago and printed in the organ of the Thomas More Book Shop, *Books on Trial*, I made an attempt at a contribution to good public argument on this difficult subject. Part of my argument consisted in stating four practical rules that should govern the action of minority groups in a pluralist society, in their legitimate efforts to improve public morality. These rules were not original. I had seen them stated in substance in a news release of a paper given at Marquette University on March 23, 1956 by Prof. Vernon J. Bourke of St. Louis University.

Mr. Fischer quotes my statement of these four procedural rules in support of certain conclusions of his own with regard to the activities of the National Organization for Decent Literature. Perhaps Mr. Bourke will undertake to say whether, and how far, Mr. Fischer's conclusions follow from the four norms of action for whose formulation, in language somewhat different from my own, he should be given the credit. (At the time of my writing there was no printed source to which I could refer the reader for Mr. Bourke's excellent paper; it has since appeared in the volume *Problems of Communication in a Pluralistic Society*, Marquette University Press, 1956.) My own major concern is with a broader question—the quality of public argument. My question is whether Mr. Fischer has made a contribution to rational public argument on the issue of censorship. I am afraid my answer must be No.

Consider the preliminary question of language. In his opening paragraph Mr. Fischer asserts that a "little band of Catholics" is "engaged in an un-American activity which is as flagrant as anything the Communist party ever attempted— and which is in fact very similar to Communist tactics." Does one open a rational public argument by two such attacks on the reason of the reader? That tired old cuss-word, "un-American activity"—has it not gone the way of all cuss-words, into meaninglessness? And the tactic of slapping the label "Communist" on your adversary's position—have we not agreed that this is a tactic of unreason? As for the later argument by epithet (the NODL is "lynching" books), one hardly expects to find it in *Harper's*, however much it may be used on the hustings.

The more substantive question is this: has Mr. Fischer done justice to the NODL's own understanding of its purposes and methods, as these are stated in its explanatory literature?

The literature is easily obtainable from the central office (31 East Congress St., Chicago 5, Ill.). On reading it, one would come, I think, to the following conclusions. The NODL is simply a "service organization," not an "action group." Its major service consists in offering to "responsible individuals and organizations an evaluation of current comic books, magazines and pocket-size books." This is the famous "NODL list." The evaluation of these types of publications (only these) is done singly from the standpoint of what is objectionable as juvenile reading. The standards of evaluation are nine in number. All of them are common-sense norms; none of them are special tenets of any type of "group morality." Methods of review vary for each type of publication. Five reviewers vote on each item. The purpose is to "encourage the publishing and distribution of good literature," as well as to discover what is unfit for adolescents.

NODL also distributes information about ways of organizing decent-literature campaigns on the community or parish levels. It is clearly stated that the list is merely an expression of a publication's nonconformity with the NODL code and that "the list is not to be used for purposes of boycott or coercion." The recommended procedures seem to rest on the suppositions that the ordinary merchant is a responsible man; that he would welcome some assistance in ridding his shop of stuff that responsible parents fairly judge to be unfit for their children; that if he accepts the assistance, he is to be commended; that if he rejects it, he is to be left alone. (NODL says: "Instruct your committee workers to leave silently if the owner, manager or clerk refuses cooperation.")

The general conclusion, on the basis of its own statements about itself, would be that the NODL looks to voluntary reform, through cooperation between parent-citizens and merchants, in an area where a special problem of public morality exists. That problem arises out of the ready accessibility to boys and girls of a rather immense amount of cheap literature that is objectionable on common-sense grounds of morality and taste.

Consider now Mr. Fischer's description of the NODL. "Its main purpose is to make it impossible for anybody to buy books and other publications which it does not like." "Its chief method is to put pressure on newsdealers, drug stores and booksellers to force them to remove from their stocks every item on the NODL blacklist." It "deliberately prefers to ignore the established legal channels for proceedings against books which it thinks improper. Its chosen weapons are boycott and literary lynching." It is embarked upon a "campaign of intimidation."

Something is wrong here. When Mr. Fischer describes the NODL he is obviously not describing the same thing that NODL describes when it describes itself. Thus you have reproduced the perfect pattern—the perfectly wretched pattern—of so much American public argument at the moment. There is really no argument at all—at least not yet. The two sides are not talking about the same thing. Hence the exchange proceeds to the customarily futile end. On the basis of his own description Mr. Fischer asserts that NODL "is *compelling* [emphasis his] readers, of all faiths, to bow to its dislikes, by denying them a free choice in what they buy." Hence he defines the issue thus: "The real issue is whether any private group—however well-meaning—has a right to dictate what other people may read."

To Mr. Fischer's charges the NODL would, I expect, reply to this effect: "But we are not compelling anybody to do or not do anything. We are not doing any such arbitrary thing as making our own 'dislikes' the coercive standard for the reading of the general public. We are not trying to do any 'dictating.' And as for denying to readers of all faiths a free choice in what they buy—that is not the real issue at all."

Thus the argument fulfils the customary American pattern. The next step is for the contestants to retire from the field, either in sorrow or in anger or in both. Thereafter their partisans move in. Epithets are bandied; labels are exchanged; *non-sequitur's* proliferate. Until finally, both sides mutter disgustedly, "So's your old man." And there is, for a time, a sullen silence.

Maybe the argument could be rescued from this dismal
end, to which most arguments in America seem to be condemned. Mr. Fischer could have rescued it, but he didn't.
The NODL could have obviated the need for rescue, but it
hasn't. The point where rescue begins is, of course, a fact.
Mr. Fischer notes the fact, but he abuses it to advance his
own purposes. The NODL must surely recognize the fact, but
it has not acted on the recognition, to the detriment of its
own purposes. The fact is that in half-a-dozen or more cities
and towns the police have made use of the NODL list in
order to threaten, coerce or punish dealers in reading matter.

Unquestionably, officers of the law have full right to use
the weapons of law, which are coercive. The point in question,
however, is their use of the NODL list. This puts NODL in
an ambiguous position. It cannot expect to have the thing
both ways. It cannot, on the one hand, protest that "the list
is not to be used for purposes of boycott or coercion," and, on
the other hand, fail to protest against the use of the list by
the police. It has to choose its cooperators—either the merchant or the police. It cannot choose both; for the choice is
really between opposed methods of cooperation—the method
of voluntary cooperation as between equal citizens, or the
method of coercion as used by the police.

If NODL consents to the use of its list by the police, it
creates an ambiguity that its critics may rightly seize upon,
as Mr. Fischer did; what is worse, it obscures from public
view its own "idea," the altogether valid idea of voluntary reform. On the other hand, if NODL does not consent to the
use of its list by the police, it should say so—publicly, and on
every necessary occasion. Surely part of its service must be
the supervision, conducted on its own principles, of the uses
to which its list is put.

There is another inappropriateness here. Officers of the law
must operate under statutes which in this matter are, or ought
to be, narrowly drawn. On the other hand, voluntary reform,
precisely because it is voluntary, may be based on the somewhat broader categories of common-sense judgment. The lat-
ter are employed by the NODL, rightly enough. But for this
very reason it is not right for the police to use NODL's judgments in enforcing the law. The law must have its own stand-

ards, minimal enough to sustain the challenge of due process.

In this connection another fact must be noted. The fact is that on NODL lists there appear some twenty-odd works that either have received literary honors or at least have been acclaimed by serious critics. Doubtless high-school teachers could not, without absurdity, make them required reading for their students. But the police cannot, without equal absurdity, make them prohibited reading. Such stultification of the law is itself immoral.

There is a third fact of some consequence. The history of censorship has been a history of excess. The NODL has the problem of the local zealot, operating far from the central office in Chicago, and way outside the four pages of sensible procedures sent out from it. He or she "has the zeal of God indeed, but not according to understanding" (Romans 10:2). Such zealots are righteous, usually indignant, people. They have a good cause. They want results. What they lack is St. Paul's "understanding," which bears, he said, on "the *way* of justification."

I shall not labor the analogy. The point of it, in our case, is that the zealot at times fails to see how his zeal for results may betray him into the use of methods that will in turn betray his cause. Mr. Fischer, for example, in his zeal for his own cause, which is a good one, fell into a bad method of argument. Among other faults, he fails to distinguish between the "idea" of the NODL, which is the substantive issue, and the applications of the idea, which raise issues of procedure. In good "liberal" fashion he assigns the primacy to the procedural over the substantive. Contrariwise, in good "Catholic" fashion, the local zealot for the NODL cause assigns the primacy to the substantive over the procedural. He, or she, wants the newsstands "cleaned up"; and he, or she, in some instances doesn't greatly care how.

At that, Mr. Fischer is more nearly right. In this sensitive area the question of procedure is all-important. Part of the service of NODL to its own cause should be what I can only call a service of fraternal correction. It should somehow find a way of rebuking, or at least disavowing, the local zealot who violates, or goes beyond, the cooperative procedures, none of them coercive, which it officially stands for. (As for Mr.

Fischer, maybe I have myself done him some service of intellectual charity?)

At this point, with all the ambiguities at least sorted out, if not cleared up, we could begin the rational public argument. The starting-point, would be a fact—the existence of a "real national problem" (Mr. Fischer's words). Then the questions arise. For instance, does Mr. Fischer adequately measure the dimensions of the problem? He says:

"A good many tawdry and disreputable magazines, paperbound reprints and comic books have been offered for sale on a lot of newsstands. A few publishers unquestionably have tried to base their sales appeal on sex and violence; the pictures and text on the covers of their publications often hint that the contents are far more salacious than they are in fact."

He adds that "law-enforcement agencies in some cities have not been vigorous in enforcing the statutes against obscene publications." And that's it.

Or is it? Others would maintain that this is an astonishing understatement of the real national problem. They see the problem much more ominously large. A major issue in public morality has arisen; the morals of youth are particularly involved in it; the problem is growing. They further see a causal line between bad magazines, etc., and immorality. And they feel it imperative to "do something" about the bad literature.

When these last statements are made, they start up the current argument between sociology and common sense. The sociologist expresses professional doubt about the causal line between bad reading and immorality; he finds insufficient evidence for it. The common-sense view asserts that the causal line is sufficiently established by the nature, content, tendency, etc., of the literature itself. At least a strong presumption is thus created; and it furnishes reason for action, until —and maybe after—all the Ph.D. theses, pro and con, have been written.

The word "action" disturbs the jealous advocate of civil rights. He therefore comes up with his own causal line—between any attempt at suppressing any kind of literature and the subversion of the foundations of the Republic. The common-sense view expresses doubt about this causal line. There is, it says, insufficient evidence that any such alarming consequences will follow, if the action taken is rational and prudent.

Here the real issue begins to appear: what kinds of action, as taken by whom, are rational and prudent in the circumstances? And what promise of effectiveness do they offer?

Mr. Fischer has his own program of action, which deserves consideration. He recommends two positive courses. The first is self-regulation by newsdealers, booksellers and other merchants. They should, he says, "set their own house in order; they should refuse to sell any publication which—in their own untrammeled judgment—falls below their own standards as responsible businessmen."

A question of fact occurs here: how effective so far has the principle of self-regulation been in the solution of our real national problem? The evidence suggests a discouraging answer. Some efforts in this direction have been made, always under the pressure of public opinion; but their slim success bases little hope for the future. Second, the principle itself may be, and has been, called in question. For instance, in a report entitled *The Freedom to Read*, written for the National Book Committee, Richard McKeon, Walter Gellhorn and Robert K. Merton say this:

"The dangers of police censorship are obvious; but we are convinced that the dangers of a code of self-censorship are even greater. It provides the means by which all kinds of restrictions can be put on freedom of expression, and it places the freedom to read in the hands of a group which does not even have the accountability to the public which a chief of police has" (p. 70).

I don't necessarily endorse this judgment; but it may suggest that Mr. Fischer is on shaky ground.

There are other questions too. What, I might ask, is the right of a newsdealer to "untrammeled judgment"? Is his judgment, as a matter of fact, untrammeled? And whether it is or not, why should one trust it as a means of solution for our real national problem? Is he a better critic of literature, a better judge of morality, than the average parent? How is one even to know what his "standards as a responsible businessman" are? And if they could be known, is there to be no possibility of public judgment on them? On what title is this Olympian immunity claimed? One would like to know.

The second positive course is the action of law—legislative and court action. I am inclined to think that Mr. Fischer's confidence in the efficacy of legal action as a corrective in this difficult field of printed media will be astonishing to students of the law. If I mistake not, it is pretty generally admitted that the present legal picture is a muddle. It is further admitted that the difficulties encountered in trying to straighten it out are immense. There are the two sacred legal doctrines that must be protected—prior restraint and due process. Furthermore, there are certain adverse high-court decisions that seem to have reduced the law to a state of practical impotence, not least in the two crucial areas of obscenity and violence.

What is even more decisive, even if the law could be lifted to the full height of its legitimate potency, it would still be largely impotent to cope with the new problem of mass media, whose crude subtleties seem to defeat the subtle crudities of the law. The grounds for accepting the relative ineffectiveness of law in this special field, where the moral issue is not justice, are both theoretical and practical—to be found both in the art of jurisprudence and in the lessons of history.

Mr. Fischer suggests two manners of action—one private, the other public—whose possibilities ought by all means be explored and exploited. But in the course of rational public argument it would, I think, appear that his program of positive action is inadequate to the real national problem that confronts us. His negative demand is more acceptable. He wants organizations of private right to stop campaigns of coercion. So do I. Mr. Fischer's reasons are, I think, doctrinaire; further argument would have to illuminate the fact, if it is a fact. Whereas, I, as a Catholic, am not a doctrinaire.

In my Chicago lecture I said that ". . . it is not possible to prove the position, taken by some, that an action like the boycott of a moving picture is somehow 'unrightful,' or 'undemocratic' or 'unconstitutional.' No one can show that such an action lies beyond the limits of a primeval American right to protest and object. The action may indeed be strenuous; but the American right to protest and object is permitted to run to some pretty strenuous extremes. This said against the doctrinaire, it remains true that methods of action which verge upon the coercive exhibit some incongruity when used by citizen-groups in the interests of morality in literature or on the screen. Even if they raise no issue of abstract right, they do raise the concrete issue of prudence, which, equally with justice, is one of the cardinal virtues."

I hold to this position now, against Mr. Fischer (I think), and also (I think) against the NODL in its present ambiguous situation—certainly in its representation by local zealots and by the secular arm of the police.

I further hold to my previous position that private agencies such as the NODL can perform an indispensable public function in the promotion of public morality—provided they understand what their function is. It is not to supplant the coercive function of the agencies of public law. It is to represent, soberly and honestly, the principle of voluntary reform, to be accomplished on the basis of social cooperation—that sincere cooperation which in America is always ready to be stimulated but often needs stimulation.

This principle of reform is altogether valid in itself. Its applications call for prudence—concretely, as I have previously said, for "men and women of prudence, who understand the art of procedure, and understand too that we are morally bound, by the virtue of prudence, to a concrete rightness of method in the pursuit of moral aims." For the rest, the rationality of this method of social reform will be understood, and its pitfalls will be avoided, if we can all somehow hold to high standards of public discussion. In this respect the editor of *Harper's* has failed. But his failure is less reprehensible than that of Catholics who miss their present opportunity— and duty—to perform the instant task, which is to inject the Catholic tradition of rationality into a mass democracy that is rapidly slipping its moorings in reason.

American Civil Liberties Union
STATEMENT ON CENSORSHIP ACTIVITY BY PRIVATE ORGANIZATIONS AND THE NATIONAL ORGANIZATION FOR DECENT LITERATURE

Throughout the United States, private organizations concerned with the morality of literature are increasingly going beyond their legitimate function of offering to their members, and calling to public attention, opinion or instruction about books, and are in effect imposing censorship upon the general public. And since any kind of censorship infringes the principle of that constitutionally guaranteed freedom of the press which protects the free exchange of ideas in our country, it is imperative that the American people be warned of the danger in which their freedom stands. In discussing this kind of censorship, we make a clear distinction between the right of all organizations to express their opinion, which we defend, and acting in such a manner as to deny those who do not agree with their opinion an opportunity to read the literature themselves.[1]

BACKGROUND OF THE PROBLEM

1. *The constitutional guarantee.* The First and Fourteenth Amendments to the United States Constitution, and the constitutions of the several states, prohibit governmental abridgment of freedom of the press. If one may read, one must be

---

[1] The ACLU's official policy statement on pressure-group censorship, adopted in 1951, states: "The ACLU defends, as being within both the letter and the spirit of the Constitution, any simple expression by any individual or group of disapproval of the contents of any book, etc., or any attempt simply to dissuade others from buying it. It recognizes as far as legal right is concerned, the use of such orderly and lawful means as peaceful and unobstructive picketing and the organization of a specific and primary boycott even when they imply some degree of coercion. However, in view of the fact that the field of communication differs significantly from the general field of industry and commerce, the Union actively opposes, as being especially contrary to the spirit of the Constitution, the use of such

able to buy; if one may buy, others must be able to print and sell.

2. *Legal basis for limiting freedom of the press.* If curbs are to be placed on freedom of the press, and these curbs must be based on a clear and present danger of a substantive evil from the publication, they can be imposed only by our courts, through full legal process. And the courts, not private literature-reviewing organizations, are the proper tribunals for determining the existence of such danger.

3. *Existing pressures for further limitation of freedom of the press.* It is an historical fact that the travail and tension of our time has adversely affected our society and raised particular problems of juvenile delinquency. We share with other Americans deep concern about this problem, which has been a problem in other ages as well, but we do not believe that it is desirable to try to cure the evil by unwise or unlawful abridgment of our civil liberties.

4. *The form now assumed by further, improper limitation of freedom of the press.* First, some state legislatures, after vigorous demands by religious and other private organizations, have passed laws so sweeping as to permit censorship of any publication which administrators of the law may disapprove of. Rhode Island and New York now prohibit the display, sale or circulation to any person under 18 of any book dealing with "illicit sex or sexual immorality." This ban could affect the *Odyssey*, half of Shakespeare, the *Divine Comedy*; the *Scarlet Letter* and parts of the Bible; Henry James' *The Turn of the Screw* was cited by the Rhode Island commission as an example of a book thought harmful to minors. In South Carolina, the legislature passed a resolution directing the removal from public libraries of "books that are inimical to the traditions of South Carolina."

Second, less formal governmental censorship is illustrated by the fact that the Detroit Police Department has made such

---

means in the following ways: (1) as pressure, or explicit threat thereof, at any time prior to the actual offering of a motion picture, etc. to the public; and (2) even after the actual offering to the public, in the form of a general or secondary boycott—designed, for example, to close a theatre entirely or to close other theatres whose proprietors ally themselves with the proprietor of the first theatre."

representations to the only two wholesalers of paperbound books and magazines in Detroit that they have agreed not to offer any magazine or paperbound book for sale in that city until it has been submitted to the police and cleared by them or in doubtful cases by the prosecuting attorney. The list of books disapproved by the prosecuting attorney for that jurisdiction has been frequently sent to the police in other cities and used as a quasi-official "banned" list. This situation displays the particularly abhorrent practice of pre-publication censorship, because, although the books have been printed, publication is not completed if there is a barrier to distribution.

Such formal and informal censorship actions by official authority violates the First Amendment. In nearly every instance where it has been possible to test the constitutional issue in a court, censorship has been defeated.

Third, a number of private groups, particularly church-related organizations have prepared blacklists, threatened and imposed general boycotts, and awarded unofficial certificates of compliance. The most active of these groups is the National Organization for Decent Literature, a group within the Roman Catholic Church established in 1938 by the Catholic bishops of the United States. In 1955, the bishops set up a National Office for Decent Literature in Chicago, in order to coordinate the work nationally. There are other religious organizations, as well as racial, labor, parent-teachers and women's groups, who also engage in censorship activity, but our attention in this statement is focused on the NODL because of the prominence it has achieved and the great influence it has wielded in removing books from circulation.

THE NATIONAL ORGANIZATION FOR DECENT LITERATURE

The NODL is a nationwide organization whose membership is largely made up of Roman Catholic laymen; it has active units in several towns and cities. The national and local membership receives guidance from officers and priests of the Roman Catholic Church. The purpose of the NODL, as enunciated by the Bishops' Episcopal Committee, was "to organize and set in motion the moral forces of the entire country . . . against the lascivious type of literature which threatens moral, social, and national life"; it has emphasized its efforts to protect youth. The NODL Code, in addition to the negative pledge of removal of "objectionable" literature, also contains the positive pledge to "encourage publishing and distribution of good literature" and "to promote plans to develop worthwhile reading habits during the formative years." To evaluate the literature of our day in terms of its suitability for youth, the NODL, at last report, uses a reading committee of mothers of the Roman Catholic faith in the Chicago area. The NODL's focus has been on magazines, comic books, and paperbound books. It should be noted that the founders of the NODL sought from the beginning to enroll non-Catholics in their efforts. The NODL, says the Bishops' Committee, "appealed to all moral forces to combat the plague of indecent literature. The NODL office was, and is, merely a service organization to coordinate activities and supply information to all interested groups regardless of race, color or creed." The NODL's instruction manual, while listing procedures for individual committees to conduct Parish Decency Crusades, invites the cooperation of non-Catholic groups in the organization of local Decent Literature Committees to carry on the NODL work; such cooperation has not thus far been widespread.

It should be emphasized beyond the possibility of misunderstanding that the ACLU does not presume to object to the NODL's advising communicants of the Roman Catholic Church about any publication. Nor does the Union see any element of censorship in the NODL's informing the general public of its opinion that certain writings are immoral. Such criticism is a right of private freedom, and must immediately be protected when threatened.

From many towns and cities, come reports of extended NODL action which constitutes nothing less than censorship of what the American people as such may read. For example:

1. Roman Catholic parish groups, armed with the NODL list, call upon booksellers (bookstores, drug stores, tobacconists, etc.) and ask that the condemned titles not be offered for sale.

2. The NODL group informs a non-complying bookseller that they will refuse to buy any goods from him, in flagrant contradiction of its own assertion that its list is "merely an

expression of a publication's non-conformity with the NODL Code, and that the list is not being used for purposes of boycott or coercion."

3. Newsdealers, druggists, and others who agree in advance not to sell anything to which the NODL objects are given monthly certificates of compliance.

4. Lists of complying, and often of non-complying, dealers are widely publicized and parishioners are strongly urged to confine their purchases of all commodities to complying dealers. Check-ups are suggested at fortnightly intervals, i.e., a private morals-police force is encouraged to come into being.

5. In many cases police, prosecuting attorneys, and military commanders on Army posts have issued instructions or orders that no books or magazines on the NODL list shall be sold within their jurisdiction, thus putting the authority of the state in the service of a private sectarian group. However, in a recent newspaper article, the Very Reverend Monsignor Thomas J. Fitzgerald, who directs the NODL work, stated, "We request government officials not to use the list . . . It is up to the courts to decide if a book is obscene."

If these were the acts of government officials, they would at once be challenged in court.[2] That they are the acts of a non-official group makes them more difficult to attack, but they are nonetheless seriously violative of the principle of freedom.

A fundamental objection to these extended activities of the NODL is that the judgment of a particular group is being imposed upon the freedom of choice of the whole community. The novel which may be thought by a committee of Catholic mothers to be unsuitable for a Roman Catholic adolescent is thus made unavailable to the non-Catholic. It is plainly necessary to challenge the NODL as keeper, by self-election, of the conscience of the whole country.

---

[2] The October 1, 1956, issue of *Publishers' Weekly* notes that the prosecutor of St. Clair County, Michigan, has officially recognized the NODL list as the guide to what publications cannot be sold in his jurisdiction. A suit has been filed in the Federal court by five publishers of paperbound books to enjoin the prosecutor from ordering two wholesale news distributors not to handle books or magazines listed by the NODL.

THE NODL BOOK LIST

The argument against censorship applies to all lawfully published books, but it is important to note that many of the authors and titles on the NODL list are considered among the most distinguished in literature. (See the appendix to this statement.)

Books by recipients of the Nobel Prize, the Pulitzer Prize, and the National Book Award have been made markedly less available to the reading public by the censorship of a private and anonymous jury acting under its own standards of morality and taste. And these are books which have been the object of responsible literary criticism and studied in hundreds of literature courses throughout the country.

The ACLU is gratified to record that Roman Catholic opinion is by no means unanimous in support of the activities of the NODL. Father John Courtney Murray, S.J. in recent public statements admirably setting the tone for national discussion of the problem, observes that: ". . . in a pluralist society no minority group has the right to impose its own religious or moral views on other groups, through the methods of force, coercion or violence." (The ACLU emphasizes that this prescription applies as well to majority groups.) Father Murray adds: "Society has an interest in the artist's freedom of expression which is not necessarily shared by the family. If adult standards of literature would be dangerous for children, a child's standard of literature is rather appalling to an adult." He questions, as we do, the use to which the NODL list is put, particularly by public authorities and local zealots who substitute "coercion for cooperation."

The American Civil Liberties Union, which has prepared this statement and solicited signatures in support, is opposed to censorship, official or private, by police authority or by the NODL or any other group. It is our conviction that the people of this country should enjoy to the fullest extent the freedom embodied in the principle of the First Amendment. Specifically, the Union intends to expose in every way it can the use of lists of books as tools of general boycott, and to intervene on behalf of writers, publishers, vendors and purchasers who have the will to explore legal avenues for the maintenance of their freedom. We reiterate, meanwhile, that we will at all times defend the right of such an organization as the NODL to express its view.

This statement is signed by the officers of the American Civil Liberties Union who thereby indicate the intention of the Union to thwart censorship. Other persons who will not necessarily take part in the action of the ACLU have appended their signatures, because of their concern with the freedom of the press and literature and their general agreement with the principles herein set forth.

NODL States Its Case*

MONSIGNOR THOMAS J. FITZGERALD

(AUTHOR'S NOTE: *During the past year the National Office for Decent Literature has been subjected to varied criticism, the most recent being that made public May 6 by the American Civil Liberties Union. Some of it, which stemmed from honest differences of opinion, received respectful consideration. Much, however, was based on false premises or misinformation. Policies were attributed to NODL which were and are foreign to its standards and procedures. This article is written to clarify NODL's position.*)

The Catholic bishops of the United States established a National Organization for Decent Literature in December, 1938. Its purpose, as enunciated by the Episcopal Committee for NODL, was "to set in motion the moral forces of the entire country . . . against the lascivious type of literature which threatens moral, social and national life."

Subsequent events have proved that the concern of the bishops was well founded. Many authorities have since voiced their apprehension at the dangers in modern objectionable literature. For example, when a Select Committee of the House of

* Reprinted from *America* by special permission.

Representatives conducted an investigation of this literature in 1952, the majority report declared:

"Pornography is big business. The extent to which the profit motive has brushed aside all generally accepted standards of decency and good taste and substituted inferior moral standards, has become not only a national disgrace but a menace to our civic welfare as well. Parents who would not tolerate salacious conversation in their homes apparently do not object to, or are unaware of, the presence of degrading types of books and magazines devoted to the same topics, whose principal appeal is to the salacious-minded."

The National Council of Juvenile Court Judges considered the problem so serious that at its 1954 national convention it adopted a resolution which not only called for legislation at all levels of government to curtail publication of such literature but also recommended that "civic consciousness be aroused in all communities through church, fraternal, civic and business organizations to secure the voluntary cooperation of merchants, magazine distributors and associations to place the value of youth above financial gain." The reason for this drastic action, according to the judges, was as follows:

"The character of juvenile delinquency has changed as a consequence of the stimulation of these publications, being no longer the thoughtless, mischievous actions of children, but is reflected in acts of violence, armed robbery, rape, torture and even homicide to which the vicious and vile publications conditioned the minds of our children."

It will be clear from the foregoing that NODL is operating in the field of public morals. Public morals are not just a private affair, nor are they wholly a matter of religious opinion. Our American society, as its inheritance from Western culture, has definite moral standards and principles which we all respect, notwithstanding our religious differences. For these moral principles men have always been willing to fight and even to die.

The welfare of man and of society rests on these principles. It would be foolish therefore to maintain that liberty must be equated with unrestrained license. Human freedoms are essentially subordinated to good morals and are safeguarded by them. A campaign for good morals is not an infringement upon freedom, but a preparation for the enjoyment of true freedom. Freedom, then, connotes not merely a right, but a duty: a duty to good morals. Just as the individual must be concerned about the public exercise of freedom, so must he be concerned about public morality.

The Christian citizen in the exercise of his freedom feels an even greater responsibility to public morals. "The Christian cannot ignore this vice which exists on our newsstands," says Dr. A. C. Miller, secretary of the Christian Life Commission of the Southern Baptist Convention. "Even though he may not be personally attracted to it, he has a Christian stewardship toward society."

That NODL might better fulfil its purposes a national office was set up in Chicago, in April, 1955. And to correct a misapprehension that often arose out of its former title, the National Organization for Decent Literature, a new name, the National Office for Decent Literature, was adopted. This new name describes more exactly the function of NODL.

This office services all organizations—civic, educational, social and religious—that voluntarily request its aid. It does not, however, attempt to direct or dictate the policies of such organizations. Each determines its own program.

NODL supplies these groups with practical information gathered from the aggregate experience of many organizations which have been actively working on a literature program. It also issues a quarterly bulletin containing current information on activities, programs and procedures throughout the country. Finally, it prints each month a list of comic books, magazines and pocket-size books which it has judged objectionable for youth. (*It has never reviewed a cloth-bound book.*) NODL concentrates upon these publications because of their availability to youth at a nominal price.

NODL does not enter the field of adult reading. Catholics already have the law of the Church, clear and binding in conscience, which forbids the reading of "*ex professo*" obscene publications. NODL's appeal to adults outside the church is to their sense of decency and their individual responsibility to the common good. Both of these should deter them from buying and reading publications which would undermine ideals of public morality, patriotism, respect for law and the sanctity of family life.

The purpose of NODL's listing of objectionable reading is clearly indicated in the title of the list: "Publications Disapproved for Youth." (This list, as well as a list of "Acceptable Pocket-Size Books for Youth," may be obtained by writing NODL, 33 East Congress Parkway, Chicago 5, Ill. Single copies are ten cents.) Publications are evaluated according to a code for youthful reading. The code deems objectionable publications which:

1) glorify crime or the criminal;
2) describe in detail ways to commit criminal acts;
3) hold lawful authority in disrespect;
4) exploit horror, cruelty or violence;
5) portray sex facts offensively;
6) feature indecent, lewd or suggestive photographs or illustrations;
7) carry advertising which is offensive in content or advertise products which may lead to physical or moral harm;
8) use blasphemous, profane or obscene speech indiscriminately and repeatedly;
9) hold up to ridicule any national, religious or racial group.

NODL believes that this code does not embody standards peculiar to Catholics, but rather that it reflects the thinking of all people interested in the ideals of youth.

Judgment on a publication is never left to one individual. Five competent reviewers (the majority of them members of the honor sorority Kappa Gamma Pi) must agree that a magazine or pocket-size book violates the code before the publication is listed as unsuitable for youth. Five mothers of grammar-school or teen-age children must pass judgment on a comic book before it is so listed.

While the majority of reviewers are Catholic, NODL does have currently a Protestant and a Jewish reviewer. It invites all Protestants and Jews who are sincerely interested in the welfare of youth to join its reviewing board.

The NODL list also carries many mature literary works, a few of them award winners, which have appeared in paperback form. These may be suitable for adult reading but have been evaluated by NODL reviewers as too advanced for the youthful mind. Ideally and practically, NODL considers that these books should be made available for adults but kept out of the hands of youth through a program of self-regulation on the part of the publishing and distributing industries.

NODL grants permission to any organization to reprint all or part of its listing. Certainly both individuals and organizations have the privilege of disagreeing with the judgment of NODL reviewers respecting specific publications. However, if a group alters the list by additions or deletions, NODL requests that its name be not connected with the revised listing.

NODL does believe that some list, compiled by competent reviewers and based on an objective code, is necessary to help parents and interested groups. Otherwise they may be guilty of snap judgments.

NODL recognizes that one of its responsibilities is to promote good reading for youth. It already had a list of acceptable comics and recently added the list of acceptable pocket-size books mentioned above. It will strive to keep both lists current. As other methods of fostering acceptable literature for youth are explored, the results will be made available.

NODL believes, however, that the fostering of good reading habits is only a partial solution to the problem of objectionable literature. Such a program can effectively cultivate a taste for good literature in but a portion of our youth. Furthermore, this program presupposes good home and school training.

The community has a responsibility also to unwanted, rejected, retarded and abnormal children and to the youth who have no taste for good literature. Placing in the hands of such youngsters publications emphasizing the lurid, the sensational, the violent adds to the burden they already have in striving to live a normal life.

These children should be protected from such publications by every legitimate and democratic means right-thinking and intelligent citizens can muster. These means certainly include recourse to law and the right of public protest within constitutional limits.

A misunderstanding of NODL's attitude toward police action demands correction. The NODL office denies that it has ever recommended or encouraged any arbitrary coercive police action. Such is not the purpose or procedure of NODL. Under existing laws in most communities, duly constituted public officials have the obligation of taking action against vendors of obscene publications. In the initial action the police power must be employed only to arrest the vendor and must be limited to a specific publication (or publications) considered obscene under the law. The final decision as to whether the law has in fact been violated lies with the courts. If the courts rule the vendor guilty, the police power may be used when necessary to enforce this judicial decision.

NODL hopes, then, that legislators throughout the country will acquaint themselves with the type of publications available to youth at neighborhood newsstands everywhere, and also with the existing laws regarding such publications. From such a study, laws may be framed which will give public officials the means necessary to restrict the worst of the objectionable publications without placing undue hardship upon the adult reader.

While advocating the enactment of adequate and constitutional legislation to remove the worst of the offensive material from the neighborhood racks, NODL at the same time reaffirms the democratic right of any citizen to protest in a legal manner against the sale of publications he considers objectionable for youth. Further, NODL defends the right of parents, teachers, pastors of souls and others charged with the welfare of youth to counsel and direct their families, their students and their flocks in these matters.

As has been noted above, in carrying out its program NODL is working in the field of public morality. This morality can be seriously damaged by the continuous reading of objectionable literature. Such reading has the power to destroy democratic ideas and ideals in young people who may never be judged delinquents but who will be the future citizens and public officials of our country.

Our democratic way of life is based upon ideals of patriotism, family integrity, justice, honesty, respect for law and for the rights of others. These ideals must be inculcated in youth if they are to be practiced in manhood. If they are destroyed in our youth during the formative years and replaced by motives of perversion, violence, brutality, disregard for law, property and country and contempt for family responsibilities, then future generations of America face an unhappy and chaotic life.

All these vile and repulsive traits of character are glorified in certain publications on neighborhood racks today. Were one to read many passages from those publications on radio or to show some of their pictures and cartoons on TV, he would be immediately cut off the air. Yet these same passages and pictures are sold to youth with impunity. NODL urges its critics to be realistic about this danger, which is a serious threat to the future security of our country.

Legislation cannot solve the problem in its entirety. It can only rid the stands of the worst of the material. A good reading program and good recreational facilities for youth will answer part of the problem, but again not all. NODL is endeavoring to fill a void.

The U.S. Bishops' Statement of 1957 on Censorship

Censorship is today a provocative and sometimes misleading word. It generates controversy by provoking those who would deny in fact any restrictions, legal or moral, upon freedom of expression. It misleads, since few approach the problems of censorship without emotion.

Obviously the state does have some power of censorship. In times of war or great national danger, few will deny it a preventive power. In normal circumstances, however, the state exercises only a punitive function, placing restraint on those who misuse liberty to deny equal or greater rights to others. The state's power of censorship is not unlimited.

Morally, the Church can and does exercise what is called censorship. This right is hers from her office as teacher of morals and guardian of divine truth. Her decisions bind her people but her sanctions upon them are only spiritual and moral. She does, nevertheless, express her judgments to all men of good will, soliciting their reasoned understanding and their freely given acceptance and support.

Most commonly in civil affairs the particular freedom that is involved in discussions of the subject is freedom of the press, not only in newspapers and other publications, but also such dramatic expression as is repressed in the theatre, motion pictures, radio and television.

MAN'S SEARCH FOR TRUTH

Because in modern times the press has been a major instrument in the development of knowledge and the chief means of its diffusion, freedom of the press is closely bound up with man's right to knowledge. Man's patient plodding ascent to the heights of truth evidences the spiritual powers given him by God and at the same time their wounding by sin. His search for truth is an enriching and ennobling experience, uniquely proper to man.

The right to know the truth is evidently broad and sweeping. Is the right to express this knowledge, whether through speech or press, equally broad? That man has a right to communicate his ideas through the spoken or written word is beyond challenge. And yet it can be recognized at the outset that expression adds a new element to knowledge. Directed as it is to others, it is an act that has social implications. Society itself must take cognizance of it. Although man must claim and hold to freedom of expression, he must also recognize his duty to exercise it with a sense of responsibility.

This is a freedom that is intimately bound up with other freedoms that man prizes. Freedom of the press is patently a key safeguard of civil liberty. Democracy does not exist without it. The day free expression of opinion is extinguished and all are constrained to fall into a single pattern of political thought and action, democracy has died.

As indispensable as is freedom of expression to us as citizens, it is no less indispensable to the Church in carrying out her mission to preach the gospel. The content of man's knowledge of God derived through the use of his native powers has been immeasurably enriched and perfected and has been given certainty by the revelation made by God to man through Jesus Christ. This knowledge has been attained not through man's effort, but through the goodness and mercy of God. It is accepted by an act of faith made with the help of divine grace. Of this deposit of revealed truth the Church is the divinely appointed custodian.

Without an unfettered means of communication, the teaching office of the Church is sorely hampered. She counts among her special blessings in our own country the important and fruitful Catholic press.

A "RATIONAL FREEDOM"

Because freedom of the press is a basic right to be respected and safeguarded, it must be understood and defended not as license, but as true rational freedom. The kind of uncritical claims for and defense of liberty which so often have been made in our day actually places that liberty in jeopardy. For this reason we feel that light must be thrown not only on its meaning, but also on its limits.

To speak of limits is to indicate that freedom of expression is not an absolute freedom. Not infrequently it is so presented. It is alleged that this freedom can suffer no curtailment of limitation without being destroyed. The traditional and sounder understanding of freedom, and specifically freedom of the press, is more temperate. It recognizes that liberty has a moral dimension. Man is true to himself as a free being when he acts in accord with the laws of right reason. As a member of society his liberty is exercised within bounds fixed by the multiple demands of social living. In the concrete this means that the common good is to be served. It will entail, among other things, a respect for the rights of others, a regard for public order, and a positive deference to those human, moral and social values which are our common Christian heritage. It is within this context that freedom of expression is rightly understood.

This recognition of limitations has been given statement in recent decisions of the Supreme Court of the United States: "We hold that obscenity is not within the area of constitutionally protected speech or press." (Roth v. United States, 77 S. Ct. 1304, Alberts v. California, 77 S. Ct. 1304–June 24, 1957.) The decisions touching on this subject are encouraging to those who have been deeply concerned over trends that threatened to destroy the traditional authority exercised by the state over expressions and displays of obscenity.

Contrary to this trend, the court has held that there is such a thing as obscenity susceptible of legal determination and demanding legal restraint; that laws forbidding the circulation of obscene literature are not as such in violation of the Constitution; that the Federal Government may ban such publications from the mail; that a state may act against obscene literature and punish those who sell or advertise it. The decisions reasserted the traditional conviction that freedom of expression is exercised within the defined limits of law. Obscenity cannot be permitted as a proper exercise of a basic human freedom. Civil enactments as well as the moral law both indicate that the exercise of the freedom cannot be unrestrained.

NEED FOR AUTHORITY SEEN

Ideally, we could wish that no man-made legal restraints were ever necessary. Thus, restraint on any human freedom would be imposed rather by one's own reason than by external authority. In any case, restraint's best justification is that it is imposed for the sake of a greater freedom. Since, however, individuals do act in an irresponsible way and do threaten social and moral harm, society must face its responsibility and exercise its authority. The exigencies of social living demand it.

In his recent encyclical of September 8, 1957, our Holy Father has spoken not only of the competence of public administrators, but also of their strict duty to exercise supervision over the more modern media of communication and entertainment—radio and television. He warns public officials that they must look on this matter not from a merely political standpoint—but also from that of public morals, the sure foundation of which rests on the natural law. What he has said applies with even greater force to the older media—the press and motion pictures—since they have been and continue to be subject to even greater abuse and supply so much of the material used in the programs presented through the more modern media. "Nor can it be asserted," Pope Pius XII writes, "that this watchful care of the state's officials is an unfair limitation on the liberty of individual citizens, for it is concerned not with the private citizens as such but rather with the whole of human society with whom these arts are being shared."

Although civil authority has the right and duty to exercise such control over the various media of communication as is necessary to safeguard public morals, yet civil law, especially in those areas which are constitutionally protected, will define as narrowly as possible the limitations placed on freedom. The one purpose which will guide legislators in establishing necessary restraints to freedom is the securing of the general welfare through the prevention of grave and harmful abuse. Our juridical system has been dedicated from the beginning to the principle of minimal restraint. Those who may become impatient with the reluctance of the state through its laws to curb and curtail human freedom should bear in mind that this is a principle which serves to safeguard all our vital freedoms—to curb less rather than more; to hold for liberty rather than for restraint.

HIGHEST PRUDENCE NEEDED

In practice the exercise of any such curbs by the state calls for the highest discretion and prudence. This is particularly true in the area of the press. For here an unbridled power to curb and repress can make a tyrant of government, and can wrest from the people one by one their most cherished liberties.

Prudence will always demand, as is true under our governmental system, that the courts be in a position to protect the people against arbitrary repressive action. While they uphold the authority of government to suppress that which not only has no social value but is actually harmful, as is the case with the obscene, the courts will be the traditional bulwark of the people's liberties.

Within the bounds essential to the preservation of a free press, human action and human expression may fall short of what is legally punishable and may still defy the moral standards of a notable number in the community. Between the legally punishable and the morally good there exists a wide gap. If we are content to accept as morally inoffensive all that is legally unpunishable, we have lowered greatly our moral standards. It must be recognized that civil legislation by itself does not constitute an adequate standard of morality.

An understanding of this truth together with the knowledge that offensive materials on the stage and screen and in publications have a harmful effect moved the Bishops of the United States to set up agencies to work in the field—for motion pictures, the National Legion of Decency; for printed publications, the National Office for Decent Literature.

The function of these agencies is related in character. Each evaluates and offers the evaluation to those interested. Each seeks to enlist in a proper and lawful manner the co-operation of those who can curb the evil. Each invites the help of all people in the support of its objectives. Each endeavors through positive action to form habits of artistic taste which will move people to seek out and patronize the good. In their work they reflect the moral teaching of the Church. Neither agency exercises censorship in any true sense of the word.

The competence of the Church in this field comes from her divine commission as teacher of morals. Moral values are here clearly involved. Her standards of evaluation are drawn from revelation, reason and Christian tradition and from the basic norms of the moral law. These are the standards on which our nation was founded and their preservation will be a safeguard to national integrity. A judgment of moral values in these areas is of prime importance to the whole nation.

Although the Church is primarily concerned with morals and not aesthetics, the two are clearly related. Art that is false to morality is not true art. While good taste cannot supply the norm for moral judgment on literature or art, yet it must be admitted that good taste will inevitably narrow the field of what is morally objectionable.

OTHER JUDGMENTS CITED

Who can deny that in modern American life there are many grave moral problems? This is not the judgment solely of the Catholic Church. When the Select Committee of the United

States House of Representatives calls pornography big business, a national disgrace and a menace to our civic welfare; when the National Council of Juvenile Court Judges attacks vicious and evil publications as a major cause of the change of juvenile delinquency from the thoughtless and mischievous acts of children into crimes of violence, armed robbery, rape, torture and even homicide; when the New York State Joint Legislative Committee at the end of its five-year survey assures us that by actual count trash and smut on the newsstands have the advantage of numbers and that those same stands reflect an acceptance of and growing concentration on lewdness—in the face of all this we can only say that we are confronted with conditions which are fraught with peril.

Through the National Legion of Decency and the National Office for Decent Literature, we Catholics give public expression to our opinion on this subject. Through these agencies we voice our concern over conditions which, tolerated, merit expression of public indignation. But we assert that our activities as carried out by these organizations cannot justly be termed an attempt to exercise censorship.

The right to speak out in favor of good morals can hardly be challenged in a democracy such as ours. It is a long-standing tradition of this country that groups large and small have given expression of their concern over injustice, political, social and economic. Their efforts, put forth within the framework of the law, have been directed toward dislodging evils against which the law itself is powerless. In many instances such efforts have made a valuable contribution to the community.

It is in full accord with this tradition that the work of the Legion of Decency and the National Office for Decent Literature is carried on. The rights these agencies seek to protect are among the most important and sacred—the right of parents to bring up their children in an atmosphere reasonably free from defilement, the right of children to be protected from grave and insidious moral danger, the right of all not to be assailed at every turn by a display of indecency. Through the work of these agencies, the Church is able to give concrete expression of her concern.

A GUIDE TO CATHOLICS

The evaluations of these agencies have been a guide to our Catholic people. At the same time, they have enlisted the support of many others who share our concern. No one can fail to be stirred by the evident desire of so many people to remedy an unwholesome situation. And surely all those who are conscious of the gravity of the problem will applaud the efforts of the Church to safeguard the moral standards of the society in which we live.

It would be most gratifying to find it unnecessary to carry on this work. One could wish that the sense of responsibility of those who write and those who produce motion pictures would make superfluous action of this nature. Past experience, however, does not permit us to look forward to a day when this sort of evaluation will no longer be called for. Far from curtailing the work of these agencies we must have them continue. Nor can we fail to be watchful over the fields of radio and television. Meanwhile, our existing agencies must be prepared to meet a continuing evil with an unremitting effort.

As a nation, we are intensely jealous of our freedoms. We are filled with pride that they have been so fully assured to us in our democracy. The reverence in which we hold our Constitution is due in great part to the care with which it has set down for all to know basic human freedoms that are inviolable. From childhood, these truths are taught us; they become the support of our adult life.

A freedom perceived in its true essence, in its exact limits, in its context of responsibility, is a freedom doubly secure; a freedom misunderstood risks becoming a freedom lost.

Signed by members of the Administrative Board, National Catholic Welfare Conference, in the name of the Bishops of the United States: EDWARD CARDINAL MOONEY, Archbishop of Detroit; SAMUEL CARDINAL STRITCH, Archbishop of Chicago; FRANCIS CARDINAL SPELLMAN, Archbishop of New York; JAMES FRANCIS CARDINAL McINTYRE, Archbishop of Los Angeles; FRANCIS P. KEOUGH, Archbishop of Baltimore; JOSEPH E. RITTER, Archbishop of St. Louis; PATRICK A. O'BOYLE, Archbishop of Washington; LEO BINZ, Archbishop

June 19, 1985

of Dubuque; KARL J. ALTER, Archbishop of Cincinnati; JOHN F. O'HARA, C.S.C., Archbishop of Philadelphia; ALBERT G. MEYER, Archbishop of Milwaukee; EMMET M. WALSH, Bishop of Youngstown; THOMAS K. GORMAN, Bishop of Dallas-Fort Worth; JOSEPH M. GILMORE, Bishop of Helena.